Hiking to History

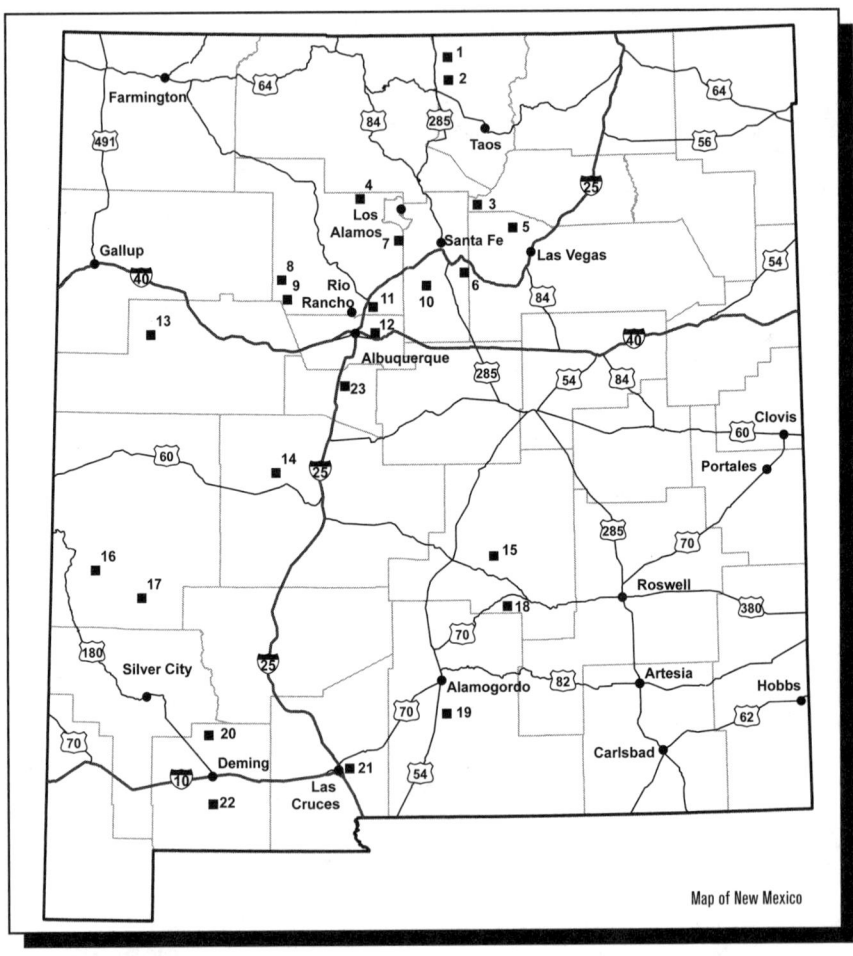

Map of New Mexico

Key to Map Numbers

1 Mount Walter	7 La Bajada	13 Airway Beacons	19 Dog Canyon
2 Sacred Site	8 Seismosaurus	14 Homesteaders	20 Cookes Canyon
3 Beattys Cabin	9 Bomb Target	15 Smokey Bear	21 Hermit Cave 2
4 Jaramillo Creek	10 Mount Chalchihuitl	16 Cooney	22 Persian Ibex
5 Hermit Cave 1	11 CCC Projects	17 Grudging Grave	23 El Cerro de Tomé
6 Battle of Glorieta	12 TWA Crash	18 Tunstall Murder	

HIKING to HISTORY

*A Guide to
Off-Road
New Mexico
Historic Sites*

Robert Julyan

University of New Mexico Press • Albuquerque

© 2016 by the UNIVERSITY OF NEW MEXICO PRESS
All rights reserved. Published 2016
Printed in the United States of America
21 20 19 18 17 16   1 2 3 4 5 6

Library of Congress Cataloging-in-Publication Data

Names: Julyan, Robert, 1943– author.
Title: Hiking to history : a guide to off-road New Mexico historic sites /
Robert Julyan.
Description: Albuquerque : University of New Mexico Press, [2016]
Identifiers: LCCN 2015030473 | ISBN 9780826356857 (pbk. : alk. paper) |
ISBN 9780826356864 (electronic)
Subjects: LCSH: Hiking—New Mexico—Guidebooks. | Trails—New Mexico—
Guidebooks. | Historic sites—New Mexico—Guidebooks.
Classification: LCC GV199.42.N6 J828 2016 | DDC 917.8904—dc23
LC record available at http://lccn.loc.gov/2015030473

Cover photograph: Harold Walter at Wheeler Peak, New Mexico, courtesy of the
Palace of the Governors Photo Archives (NMHM/DCA), 182943

Designed by Lisa C. Tremaine
Composed in Cone & Carter Galliard and Bertold Akzidenz Grotesque

*To Olivia and Emily,
that they might come to love hiking and history
as their grandfather has, and to their father,
James Holland,
who already has attained such love.*

CONTENTS

ACKNOWLEDGMENTS ix
INTRODUCTION xi

Chapter One	Mount Walter	1
Chapter Two	The Sacred Site of Taos Artists	9
Chapter Three	Beattys Cabin: Heart of the Pecos	17
Chapter Four	New Mexico's Hermit	25
Chapter Five	Jaramillo Creek: Where Plate Tectonics Came Together	33
Chapter Six	The Battle of Glorieta Pass	41
Chapter Seven	La Bajada: Every Automobile's Worst Nightmare	51
Chapter Eight	Mount Chalchihuitl	57
Chapter Nine	The Story of Sam the Dinosaur	67
Chapter Ten	Bomb Targets on New Mexico's Mesas	77
Chapter Eleven	The Crash of TWA Flight 260	83
Chapter Twelve	The Civilian Conservation Corps in the Sandias	91
Chapter Thirteen	El Cerro de Tomé	99

Chapter Fourteen	Airplane Beacons: A Pathway through the Sky 107	
Chapter Fifteen	Homestead Canyon: Land of Hope and Broken Dreams 117	
Chapter Sixteen	Smokey Bear: America's Favorite Celebrity	129
Chapter Seventeen	John Tunstall's Murder: The Shot Heard 'Round Lincoln County 141	
Chapter Eighteen	Dog Canyon 151	
Chapter Nineteen	Waylaid: The Grave of William Grudging	163
Chapter Twenty	Cooney: Miners and Apaches in the Gila Country 171	
Chapter Twenty-One	The Boneyard: Cookes Canyon 181	
Chapter Twenty-Two	Persian Ibex in New Mexico 195	

AFTERWORD   203

TO LEARN MORE   207

ACKNOWLEDGMENTS

Bill Baxter, Galisteo Basin historian
Denise Bleakly, master geographer and longtime good friend
Baldwin G. Burr, historian of the Rio Abajo and secretary of the Historical Society of New Mexico
Eddie Collins, neighbor and hunter
Mike Coltrin, hiking guide
Jan Cummings, friend, archaeology and geology maven
Jean and David Cunningham, Smokey Bear Museum, Capitan
Scott Denning, author and librarian, history maven
Fraser Goff, University of New Mexico geologist
Elise Gomber, Ruidoso River Museum
Melissa Howard, friend, Sandia Mountains maven
Steve Irwin, airway beacons expert
Michael Kamins, KNME
Jim Koehler, author and aviation maven
Tim Livingstone, retired Forest Service ranger, Capitan
Joe Dan Lowry, Turquoise Museum in Albuquerque
Tom Lyttle and Donna Smith, archaeology volunteers, Jemez Ranger District
Frances Joan Mathien, archaeologist, turquoise expert
Homer Milford of Albuquerque, a true friend of Cerrillos Hills State Park
Needa Murphy, Taos art historian

ACKNOWLEDGMENTS

Gretchen Obenauf, Bureau of Land Management archaeologist, Rio Puerco Field Office
David Pike, friend, author of *Roadside New Mexico: A Guide to Historic Markers*
Mike Prewitt, technical consultant
Greer Price, director, New Mexico Bureau of Geology
Clayton Roberts, REI, hiking and history maven
Ana Steffen, archaeologist, Jemez Ranger District
David Straub, photographer, aviation maven
Jerry Thompson, historian, author of *A Civil War History of the New Mexico Volunteers and Militia*, who shared his text and maps
Carla Ward, friend and relative, mayor of Tinkertown
Norman Ware, copyeditor
David Warnack, district ranger, Smokey Bear Ranger District
Darrell Weybright, assistant chief, Wildlife Management Division, New Mexico Department of Game and Fish
Jerold Widdison, friend, history and geography maven
Sarah Wood, New Mexico State Parks

All the people at the University of New Mexico Press, especially Clark Whitehorn, executive editor. Unflaggingly cheerful, encouraging, and helpful, they've always been a pleasure to work with.

I owe special gratitude to Richard Melzer, a good friend and a great historian, who reviewed the manuscript and whose exhaustive knowledge of New Mexico history made it a much better book. He also is a skilled writer whose many books are essential reading for anyone interested in New Mexico history.

I also am especially grateful to David Ryan, whose book *The Gentle Art of Wandering* epitomizes finding history in the New Mexico backcountry and who supplied many photos, along with his three adventure dogs, Petey, Paddy, and Teddy, accompanied me on many of my hikes.

INTRODUCTION

I've always felt that history is best experienced on foot, if for no other reason than that was usually how it was made. Not much history was made careening down a highway. And, for the same reason, I have a special fondness for historic sites beyond the reach of automobiles, because motor vehicles have a way of tainting or at least altering everything they touch, whether through parking lots, visitors' centers, roadways, or just traffic noise.

So when I moved to New Mexico more than thirty years ago, I was elated by what I found here: a wealth of historic sites from more than thirteen thousand years of human habitation located on vast tracts of wild land with limited or no road access. I came across sites on remote mesas where Paleo-Indians once hunted mammoths, and I visited deep canyons where battles had been fought. It was the stuff of high drama and romance, with colorful characters from enormous dinosaurs to Apache warriors to Billy the Kid to World War II bomber pilots.

And best of all, for me at least, many sites of historic significance could only be visited on foot. Think of Kansas or Mississippi or New Jersey or almost any state east of the hundredth meridian. They also have a plethora of historic sites, but almost all can be reached in a vehicle.

So what? you might ask. Well, for one thing, a historic site accessible only by foot is more likely to be as it was when the historic event occurred there—pristine, uncluttered, no visitors' center, no

INTRODUCTION

parking area, no interpretive or regulation signs—just you and the place and the history, closer to the event physically and emotionally. Interpretive facilities can be useful, but for me understanding history is partly an exercise in imagination, trying to see in my mind's eye what happened at the place, and that becomes easier without the overlay of interpretation.

In such circumstances, the history becomes more immediate. It's one thing to read about the Apache–US Army battles in Dog Canyon in the Sacramento Mountains and to look at the murals in the visitors' center at the canyon's mouth; it's another to hike into the canyon using the same rough trail used by the soldiers and Indians, scanning the boulder-strewn hillsides and cliffs for ambush sites. What would *I* have done if an attack had occurred *here*? Or perhaps, to see it from the Apaches' perspective: Would this be a good place from which to hurl down boulders on the white intruders? And if they pursued, could I escape?

Visiting a historic site on foot also puts us closer to the natural feeling of the event. As a Zen master would say, history happened on a day *just like this*. A day with weather, hot or cold, with clouds in the sky or clear, windy or calm, with birds making a living among the leaves, with insects going about their business, including bothering us. Or with snow on the ground, cold and wet. A day just like this. A visitors' center insulates us from these elements.

Thus, this book seeks not only to present the historic details and significance of the sites it describes but also to convey what it feels like to be there.

Not Exactly a Hiking Guide

This book is not intended to be a hiking guide, but I'd be pleased if it inspired you to visit the sites yourself. To do so, you should obtain topographic and other maps covering the site and consult sources such as the Forest Service, the Bureau of Land Management, the National Park Service, and others. I've attempted to present here minimal but sufficient information for getting to a site, including GPS coordinates (see below). With these and a good map, you should be able to find all the sites.

GPS Coordinates

Many if not most hikers today carry Global Positioning System (GPS) units, and as this book will be used, at least in part, as a guide, I've provided GPS coordinates for destinations, trail junctions, trailheads, parking areas, springs, and other features as appropriate. Unless specified otherwise, the coordinates conform to the North American Datum (NAD) 27 and are in degrees-minutes-seconds format.

How Did I Select the Sites?

This book makes no pretense to being a comprehensive compendium of off-road historic sites in New Mexico. I created my list from my own knowledge and imagination and from suggestions from generous and knowledgeable friends. I had no idea how many history and geography mavens I knew.

I wanted each site to have a story behind it, and preferably one not generally known. I wanted to tell these stories. I tended to define history broadly, which allowed me to include important or interesting events that wouldn't normally appear in a New Mexico history book, events like the discovery of *Seismosaurus*, geological measurements that confirmed plate tectonics, and World War II bomb targets. Learning about these events was fun for me, and I hope will be for you, too.

I had other criteria. A site had to be accessible to the public; if there are land-ownership issues involved, I explain in the text.

A site should be resistant to theft and vandalism. Thus I've included no archaeological sites, because they are especially vulnerable.

INTRODUCTION

I did not set distance limits. One person's stroll is another's expedition, especially if the person has physical limitations. In fact, a couple of sites can be reached by vehicle, but only if the driver is a vehicle abuser.

New Mexico is filled with amazing and interesting places, but to be included here, something of historic significance had to have *happened* at the site. It's always interesting to note that many of the most interesting and important events occurred in the most ordinary settings. The Sacred Site north of Taos and the Tunstall murder site come to mind. I did not winnow for scenery.

Occasionally, I encountered resistance to my revealing the location of a site. This was especially true with the Sacred Site near Taos. "If anyone can go to it, it will destroy the mystique"; or, "People will overrun the site and trash it." As someone who writes hiking guides, I'm familiar with this reaction, and with history sites as well as hiking sites, my reaction is the same: my first responsibility is to my readers. Sure, I don't want to make any site vulnerable to theft or vandalism, but as for being overrun, we should be so lucky. The sad truth is that far fewer people actually visit a place I've written about than people suspect—or than I would wish. Also, often the best way to protect a site is to encourage public awareness of it, and thus encourage more people to take responsibility for it.

Thus, the sites in this book are from my own idiosyncratic list. You might compile a different list, and if you do I hope you'll share it with me. In New Mexico there's plenty of off-road history to go around. Thus I encourage you to use this book as a starting point for exploring further the history and natural environment of New Mexico. I've never reached the bottom of the gold mine that is our state; you won't either.

CHAPTER ONE

Mount Walter

YOUR HIKE IS almost over. Just ahead you can see the summit of Wheeler Peak, less than half a mile more of easy walking over lichen-covered cobbles and above-timberline tundra, fewer than 28 feet of climbing to reach the top of New Mexico's highest mountain. Each state has a high point, and Wheeler Peak is especially worthy of its distinction because its 13,161 feet make New Mexico the nation's fifth-highest state, behind only Alaska, California, Colorado, and Washington. Reaching this state high point is a milestone almost obligatory for every New Mexico hiker. Ahead is Wheeler's summit cairn, usually with a cluster of other hikers, taking photographs and indulging the yellow-bellied marmots who hang out there cadging snacks.

But first you must hike over a small prominence labeled "Mount Walter" on maps, where a plaque commemorates Harold D. Walter, "who loved these mountains." It's worth pausing here to give a modicum of respect to Mount Walter, too, for while at 13,133 feet Mount Walter technically is New Mexico's second-highest mountain, it usually isn't recognized as a summit separate from Wheeler

CHAPTER ONE

The Mount Walter summit sign honoring Harold Walter. Photo by Robert Julyan.

Peak. It's only two-fifths of a mile north of Wheeler and only 28 feet lower in elevation. Mike Butterfield, in *New Mexico's High Peaks: A Photographic Celebration*, his authoritative book about New Mexico summits 12,000 feet or higher, puts it second in the list of summits but says that it doesn't qualify as being "sovereign" because it lacks the criterion of having at least a 100-foot shoulder drop from its neighbor.

Walter, the Santa Fe mountaineer, photographer, and amateur geologist who whimsically named the subsidiary summit for himself, knew better than anyone that his mountain wasn't a major summit, despite the commemorative name and the plaque. Besides, one can argue that the true memorial to Walter is Wheeler Peak itself, because Wheeler also didn't get the respect it deserved—until Walter came along.

Throughout most of New Mexico's history and into the

mid-twentieth century, if you had asked anyone what was New Mexico's highest point, without hesitation and with full confidence they'd have answered Truchas Peak, or more specifically South Truchas. An imposing summit easily seen from throughout the region, at 13,102 feet Truchas dominates the Santa Fe Mountains and the Pecos Wilderness.

Wheeler Peak, on the other hand, is tucked away in the Taos Mountains, not conspicuous from any direction. People driving north of Taos look east and assume that the towering peak they see is Wheeler, but in fact they're looking at Pueblo Peak, which is certainly no slouch at 12,305 feet but is still 800 feet lower than Wheeler.

Even Major George M. Wheeler, who between 1871 and 1876 was in charge of surveys west of the hundredth meridian and whose men, if not Wheeler himself, had climbed the mountain, did not believe that Wheeler was the highest. He was unaware that the peak named for him had that distinction.

Then along came Walter. He made his living as an accountant, but his real passions were riding horses into the Pecos Wilderness, hiking, and climbing tall peaks. And outdoor photography. His photos appeared twice on the cover of *New Mexico Magazine*, and his photos of the burned Smokey Bear cub were distributed nationwide and helped make the cub a national celebrity.

Everyone knew Walter as an outdoor adventurer. Elliott Barker (see chapter 3), in his book *Beatty's Cabin*, devoted an entire chapter to Walter, telling of his Pecos adventures. Anyone who has backpacked will recognize the victories and contretemps Walter experienced.

In the penultimate paragraph of Barker's chapter, Walter exults at having climbed South Truchas Peak. Even though he and his partner rode horses and used pack animals much of the way, it was still a noteworthy achievement. While descending, they were pummeled for two miles as they led their horses through a hailstorm with stones a half inch in diameter.

CHAPTER ONE

It was a long, tiresome trip back to the ranch, but, in spite of our exhaustion, we felt a glow of satisfaction in the fact that we had climbed the highest peak in the state, 13,300 feet. At that time that elevation was an accepted fact, and the Truchas Peaks were considered to be the highest in New Mexico. Since then, I have had no small part in having the elevations rechecked and it has been found that South Truchas is actually 13,110 feet and that Wheeler Peak in the Taos Mountains is slightly higher.

It's impossible to read Walters's account and not feel his exuberant passion for the mountains. Years after his death I met his widow, May Walter, who lived in Santa Fe. In her living room she spoke of her husband and proudly displayed the black-and-white photos he had taken. I thought of when they had been taken, of the happy days spent on mountaintops and high ridges, beside Pecos Wilderness lakes and streams, of the love for the wilderness that went into them.

After Walter's death in 1958, a previously unnamed prominence just north of Wheeler's summit was officially named Mount Walter, a name Walter himself had begun using. A plaque on the summit commemorates Walter, "who loved these mountains."

I'm someone who studies geographic names (see *The Place Names of New Mexico*); I don't think Wheeler Peak is a particularly bad (or particularly good) name for the state's highest mountain. It's certainly better than Mount McKinley, until recently the name of North America's highest summit, which was named by a disgruntled prospector because he favored the Ohio senator's position (McKinley wasn't yet president) on the free silver issue (you remember that, don't you?). Almost everyone agrees that the majestic summit should be named Denali, the native Athabascan name meaning "great one," but the Ohio congressional delegation had blocked efforts to change the name of their favorite son on the Alaskan peak. In 2015, however, President Barack Obama, by executive order, changed the name to Denali, the name the mountain should have had all along.

MOUNT WALTER

Harold Walter on the summit of Wheeler Peak. Courtesy of the Palace of the Governors Photo Archives (NMHM/DCA), 182943.

Major Wheeler, unlike McKinley, at least had the opportunity to see the peak named for him, and he was an important figure in western history and geography. But he probably didn't climb it—and, besides, several other summits in the West are named for him, including three Wheeler Peaks in California, the highest being 11,630 feet; Wheeler Peak, 13,054 feet, in Nevada; and 2,657-foot Wheeler Peak in Alaska, as well as 13,645-foot Wheeler Mountain in Colorado.

While I'm not fond of commemorative names, I do feel that the name Mount Walter is a good one, for whenever I stand atop the rise it labels and read the plaque, I'm inspired to feel some of the same love for these mountains that Harold Walter felt standing in the same place. What a fitting memorial.

CHAPTER ONE

The Hike

To reach the summits of Wheeler Peak and Mount Walter (N 36 33 39 / W 105 24 51) isn't particularly difficult—or particularly easy—and should be on the must-do list of everyone who loves New Mexico's outdoors. Most hikers take one of two routes. The shortest, and most difficult, begins at Taos Ski Valley and follows Lake Fork Valley for 3.5 miles toward Williams Lake (N 36 33 24 / W 105 25 43), a shallow but scenic tarn at Wheeler's western base. Before reaching the lake, a sign points toward the Wheeler Peak Trail, which ascends approximately one mile via switchbacks to the ridge north of Walter and Wheeler. This is the route preferred by hikers who want to get up and down as expeditiously as possible, for instance during the summer monsoon season and its lightning storms.

The other route also begins at Taos Ski Valley. It follows a dirt road east for about 1.8 miles to Bull-of-the-Woods Pasture (N 36 36 43.5 / W 105 25 42), where it heads south. En route, it meets the Blue Lake Trail and descends into La Cal Basin before climbing back onto the ridge leading to Wheeler, but most hikers prefer not to descend and instead follow contour lines as they continue on toward Wheeler, passing over 12,163-foot Frazer Mountain. From Bull-of-the-Woods Pasture to Wheeler Peak by the most direct route is 4.8 miles one way.

Another Peak Belatedly Recognized

Wheeler Peak isn't the only major mountain whose preeminence was not immediately recognized; consider Mount Everest. Until the mid-nineteenth century, Chimborazo, the huge stratovolcano in Ecuador, was believed to be the world's tallest mountain.

The problem wasn't that Everest was mistakenly judged to be lower but rather that remoteness had prevented the Himalayan giants from being measured accurately. Explorers knew that the peaks they were encountering could challenge Chimborazo, but how could they prove it?

A yellow-bellied marmot, a year-round resident on Mount Walter and Wheeler Peak. Photo by Patrick McCarthy.

Then along came George Everest, who, at age thirty-three, had been appointed superintendent of the Survey of India. He was renowned for his sophisticated methods and high standards of accuracy. In 1849 the first observations of Everest, then known only as Peak XV, were recorded. As I explained in *Mountain Names* (Seattle, WA: Mountaineers Books, 1984), "That obscurity ended one day in 1852 when the head of the computing office of the Survey of India, Radhanath Sikhdar, burst breathlessly into the office of the surveyor general, Sir Andrew Waugh, and announced, 'Sir, I have discovered the highest mountain in the world!' A check of the six stations from which Peak XV had been observed confirmed this judgment; the mean height was 29,002 feet / 8,840 meters, later corrected to the present figure [29,029 feet / 8,848 meters]."

Three years later, at a meeting of the Royal Geographical Society in London, Waugh proposed naming Peak XV for his predecessor,

CHAPTER ONE

Sir George Everest, and the society, ignoring the long-standing Nepali and Tibetan names for the mountain, agreed.

All was not lost for Chimborazo, however. Because it is located on the equatorial bulge, it remains the mountain farthest from the center of the earth.

To Learn More

Read *The Mountains of New Mexico*, by Robert Julyan (Albuquerque: University of New Mexico Press, 2006), which has much information about the entire Sangre de Cristo Mountains and their subranges, including hiking information.

Read *New Mexico's High Peaks: A Photographic Celebration*, by Mike Butterfield, foreword by Robert Julyan (Albuquerque: University of New Mexico Press, 2014). The photographs are as impressive as the mountains themselves, and the text includes much interesting and useful information.

CHAPTER TWO

The Sacred Site of Taos Artists

ARTISTS AND ART historians in Taos call it the Sacred Site, because that's "where everything changed." In 1898 two young New York City artists, Ernest L. Blumenschein and Bert Phillips, on a quest for a fresh vision for painting, had come west. They first went to Denver, where they outfitted a two-horse wagon, and then they headed south, intending ultimately to arrive in Mexico. But on a rough dirt road in northern New Mexico, in the western foothills of the Sangre de Cristo Mountains, fate, providence, or chance (depending on your spiritual orientation) intervened. A wagon wheel broke, stranding them. The nearest place to repair it was Taos, some twenty miles away.

They flipped a three-dollar gold coin to see who would go, while the other stayed with the wagon. Blumenschein lost, so he got on a horse, hoisted up the broken wheel, and headed south.

What he found as he rode the horse over the northern Taos plain was an unexpected landscape of "beauty of color, vigorous forms, and ever-changing light." He was enchanted.

CHAPTER TWO

Bert Phillips and the broken-down wagon. Courtesy of the Palace of the Governors Photo Archives, 040377.

When he and Phillips returned to Taos with the repaired wagon, they realized they had found the new vision they were seeking. As Phillips later recalled, "We abandoned the idea of going to Mexico, so we sold the wagon and horses and moved into an adobe house. Then and there began the Taos art colony, now famous all over the world."

So the place where the wagon broke down, sending Blumenschein into Taos, is legitimately called the Sacred Site. I set out to find it.

Years ago my friend and an expert on the Taos Society of Artists, Robert R. White, had told me he'd found the Sacred Site, a term he used, but when I recently asked him for its location, he was too ill to communicate the directions.

But I was certain he wasn't the only Taos art expert who knew the site's location, so I called the Harwood Foundation, the Center for Southwest Research at the University of New Mexico–Taos, and the Blumenschein Home and Museum. Most said they'd check around and call me back. They didn't. I had the distinct impression they'd just as soon I forgot about the project.

One person let slip that the site was on the Old Lama Road. Another suggested I watch the KNME production *Painting Taos*, about the history of the Taos art colony. I obtained a copy from a friend at KNME, and sure enough, the film opened with a pilgrimage to the Sacred Site. It showed an art historian hiking uphill through the woods to a large, white boulder. No road was visible in the film, but I could see in the background a mountain profile; if I could match that, I should be close.

I had other clues. Blumenschein and Phillips had documented the incident with photographs of the road, the broken wagon, and a conspicuous large white rock beside the road. That rock, about the size of a large suitcase, was the definitive marker for the site. It appeared in photos the two artists took of their broken wagon and also in the film.

One last call. The woman at the Blumenschein Museum said, "Go to San Cristobal, head toward the mountains, turn left—and you're on your own." Make a left at the mountains—not exactly GPS coordinates, but curiously it was all I needed to put everything in place.

I found on a map what I believed was the Old Lama Road. I expected to hike most of the way—after all, that was what the film implied—so after a short drive on what was a surprisingly good dirt road, I parked and started walking.

I immediately plunged into the woods, reasoning that the old road had gone back to forest and brush. I found numerous faint tracks, but each soon petered out. Time to get back on the main dirt road and look for the mountain profile.

Almost as soon as I did that, the mountains seemed to be lining up. The road began going downhill, as I knew it must.

And then, to my left, was another dirt road, not as well traveled as the one I was on but nonetheless an obvious old road, such as the Old Lama Road would have been. After all, for years the road had

CHAPTER TWO

been the main route between Lama and San Cristobal, which was why Blumenschein and Phillips had chosen to travel it.

I hiked two hundred yards down this road, the walking easy and gentle over a carpet of pine needles, the mountain profile increasingly looking like the profile in the photos, when suddenly I saw beside the road a large, white rock, precisely where it should be if this truly was the site. I whipped out the photos I had of the rock, taken by the artists and also by the film crew. I looked at distinctive bumps and cracks on the rock. They all matched. This was it. I had found the Sacred Site.

Now to be sure, this was no Black Stone of the Ka'aba in Mecca, no Stone of Scone (aka the Destiny Stone or Coronation Stone) in Britain, no Rosetta Stone from Egypt, no Blarney Stone in Blarney, Ireland, no Rock of Cashel in County Tipperary. But let's face it: an object's significance usually has more to do with human interpretations than innate appearance. The Sacred Site's "Stone of Taos" is just an ordinary, large, white rock, one of tens of thousands scattered throughout the forest. Certainly Blumenschein and Phillips didn't think it anything special. For all I know, they may have cursed at it for causing the wheel to break. Or perhaps it was just another big white rock, convenient for sitting on, nothing more.

But ever since, it has marked the site where an unforeseen concatenation of events was set in motion "that changed everything." So I am willing to grant the stone its sacredness.

I photographed it and took GPS coordinates to mark its location. I basked in my discovery. Kit Carson, Old Bill Williams, and other early explorers would have been proud of me, even though I had used modern maps and a GPS unit. I took more photographs of the rock and the road. Then I began hiking back to my car.

On the way, however, troubling issues arose. If the site was on an obvious old road, why had the art historian made it seem that it could be reached only by hiking through the forest? And why had the film crew kept the road out of their footage?

I knew the answer: while *they* knew the site's location, and that it

THE SACRED SITE OF TAOS ARTISTS

Ernest Blumenschein taking the broken wagon wheel to Taos. Courtesy of the Palace of the Governors Photo Archives, 040379.

was easily reached, they didn't want it revealed to anyone else, certainly not the public at large. Later, a woman at the Blumenschein Museum put it succinctly: if the site were widely known, it could be overrun. She allowed that she'd never been to the site herself, but she was not dissuaded when I said that it was not the sort of place that would attract tour buses.

Actually, her real reason for not wanting the site's location publicized was that the loss of secrecy would detract from the site's "mystique."

Mystique is big in Taos—and northern New Mexico in general—especially among sensitive souls, of whom I count myself one. Mystique tugs as hard on me as well. I've always been an aficionado of lost-mine stories, and I'd be profoundly resentful and disappointed if someone announced they'd found the Lost Dutchman Mine in the Superstition Mountains and it turned out to be just a little hole with worthless pyrite scattered around. Trashing mystique is not something I take lightly.

CHAPTER TWO

The Sacred Site and the big, white rock as they appear today. Photo by Robert Julyan.

But there was still something fundamentally unfair about a small cadre of in-group specialists deciding who should visit the site and who should not. The site is on public land, Carson National Forest; in a deep and literal sense, it belongs to all of us. And something of significance to all of us did happen there. If someone cares enough about Taos art history to want to see where it all began, then they should be able to do so without obstruction.

Another reason for recognizing the site's location is to preserve it. Not that I expect vandals could do much harm to the big, white rock, but as my short hike proved, the Forest Service and local road crews have been continually grading and improving roads in the area. A person with a bulldozer grading the Old Lama Road might come to the big white rock and push it down the hill.

What should I do?

After much temporizing, I finally concluded that the site's greatest threat was not human vandals but rather road crews ignorant of the site's significance. The more people who know about the site, the more it will be protected.

Here are directions for getting to the Sacred Site. At the end of this route description, I have included GPS coordinates, but try to use them only as a last resort; have some fun searching. I also am including photographs of the stone and the mountain profile. This means that you, dear reader, should be able to find it, but also that you might have to look for it, as I did. And that was the adventure. Besides, we tend to value objectives more if we've had to work for them.

Drive along US 64 north from Taos to its junction with NM 522. Continue north on this for just over ten miles to where a good dirt road branches east to the village of San Cristobal. Follow this main road into the village and look for Camino del Medio, a dirt road that goes through the village before bending northeast to enter the forest. Numerous old dirt roads intersect in the forest. The coordinates for the junction of Camino del Medio and the Old Lama Road leading to the big white rock are provided below. You could begin hiking anywhere along Camino del Medio and have a pleasant walk in the Sangre de Cristo foothills. When you find the Old Lama Road, not signposted and ungraded, follow it as it gently descends about 0.14 miles to the big white rock on your left and the Sacred Site.

What you do next is up to you. Take photos, have a picnic, remember Blumenschein and Phillips, or, best of all, reflect upon the power of serendipity and providence in all our lives.

Then, as you drive back to Taos, look around and see what Blumenschein saw, and remember that he wasn't looking through the window of a rapidly moving car but rather was riding a slow-moving horse. The vastness of the Taos plain, the majesty of the Sangre de Cristos, the preternatural clarity of the sky, the vividness of colors. Allow yourself to be moved as Blumenschein and later Phillips were moved. Then think about how you were brought to this moment by the power of a random white rock on a rough old road.

A sacred site indeed.

CHAPTER TWO

The GPS Coordinates

The junction of Camino del Medio and the Old Lama Road is at N 36 37 01.5 / W 105 36 57. Allow for some leeway on the longitude. The Old Lama Road does not appear on topographic maps, but it is visible on Google Earth. The big white rock is at N 36 37 08 / W 105 36 57.

CHAPTER THREE

Beattys Cabin
Heart of the Pecos

IN HIS BOOK *Beatty's Cabin*, Elliott Barker described his first visit to the heart of what is now the Pecos Wilderness. It was 1896; he was ten years old and living with his family on their ranch on the Sapello River east of the wilderness. His father and other men were planning a hunting and fishing trip—without Elliott. He was distraught. He raced around "bellerin' and blubberin'," pleading to go along, until his father, with extreme reluctance, said, "Ok, if your mom says it's all right you can go." I don't imagine Ma Barker had a choice, given the onslaught of words she faced from her son, and she probably was happy to be rid of him. And so Elliott mounted a huge mule and headed off with the others into the Pecos high country.

    I cannot read his account of that wondrous life-changing trip without recalling a similar experience I had when I was about the same age, going with two uncles, one an old miner and prospector, on a fishing expedition to Heart Lake, a high-country tarn in what is now the Indian Peaks Wilderness in Colorado's Front Range. There are many differences in the details between my trip

CHAPTER THREE

The cover of Elliott Barker's book about the Pecos Wilderness.

and Elliott's. Elliott rode a mule, while I hiked with a crude, homemade backpack. They stayed a long time; we were gone but two nights. They hunted and fished; we just fished. The decaying landmark they found was Beattys Cabin; ours was a decaying log structure called the Jenkins Sawmill.

But with Barker as with me, the experience changed our lives. When he got married, he took his new bride to the Pecos Wilderness. Even late in old age—he lived to be 101—he continued his love affair with the region. And I have never outgrown my love of the Rocky Mountain high country; likewise, soon after my wife and I were married, I took her backpacking to the same high-country lake I had hiked to as a youth.

My motive in this personal digression is my hope that, among my readers, a few might consider taking a son or daughter on a similar life-changing excursion into the wilderness—and perhaps that trip could be to Beattys Cabin.

First, make no mistake: there's no cabin at Beattys Cabin. Perhaps you'll find a Forest Service cabin, but the original Beattys Cabin is long gone. Even in Barker's time, the cabin was decaying.

When I first saw the cabin [seven years after first exploring the Pecos], more than 50 years ago [as of 1953], it had been abandoned, and the dirt roof was beginning to cave. Now there is left only a little heap of earth and stone where the fireplace once stood. But the place is still known as "Beattys Cabin" and it is the most noted spot in the entire Pecos Wilderness area, now having come to mean the general locality. A hunter or a fisherman can say he is packing into Beattys Cabin, yet pitch his tent anywhere within a radius of two or three miles of the spot where the cabin stood. The US Forest Service and State Game Department administrative cabins, now located just across the creek, also are referred to as Beattys Cabin.

Barker knew personally the man who had built the cabin and who used it as a base for his activities in the wilderness. George Beatty sometimes stopped at the Barker Ranch on the Sapello, and thus the young Elliott met him:

We kids thought his distinctive mustache and little goatee ridiculous and funny, but we listened wide-eyed to his wild tales of adventures in the mountains and how he had been on the verge of striking a gold mine. . . . He sometimes spoke of his cabin on the upper Pecos River, referring to it as his "ranch," but even then, I am sure, he had completely abandoned it.

In his book, Barker referred to an account of Beatty and his cabin by Lewis Lindsay (L. L.) Dyche, a naturalist with the University of Kansas, who made three specimen-collecting trips to northern New Mexico, bringing back insects and birds but also some large mammals—whitetail and mule deer, elk, mountain lions, and black and grizzly bears. One suspects that it was as much a hunting trip as a scientific endeavor, but in the early 1880s that was what

CHAPTER THREE

people back east wanted to see—specimens of fierce wild animals like grizzlies. Dyche described Beatty's goatee, his foot-long bear knives, his storytelling "flavored with typical mountaineer profanity," and his cabin on the Upper Pecos. Sadly, by the time of Beatty and Dyche and certainly Barker, the large mammals they hunted were already in decline.

The hunters of Barker's 1896 hike certainly would have been disappointed if they scanned the forests for elk. By 1888, elk were extinct in the Pecos. They'd have kept a wary eye out for grizzly bears (*Ursus horribilis*), but even then the Pecos grizzlies had but twenty-seven more years in the Pecos; the last one was shot in 1923. (The last grizzly in the state was killed on Rain Creek in southwestern New Mexico in 1935.)

And it was not hunters such as Dyche and the Barkers and Beatty and others like them who killed off the big game in the Pecos. It was market hunting: the wholesale slaughter of game to sell as meat to local and out-of-state markets. Few people today can imagine that many of New Mexico's iconic animals were gone by the end of the frontier period. As mentioned above, elk were gone from the Pecos by 1888, and by 1900 they were gone from the rest of the state. Rocky Mountain bighorn sheep were also gone by 1900. Pronghorns persisted in just a few herds on the plains. Perhaps the most telling example of the extent of wildlife devastation is that during the 1915 hunting season, on the one million acres of Carson National Forest (which includes much of the Pecos Wilderness), only eight deer were taken.

No one felt the loss more than Barker, and he spent much of the rest of his long career working to restore what had been lost. In 1915 a herd of Gunnison's elk were brought in from Wyoming. Genetically distinct from the local elk, they nonetheless took hold and thrived, but meanwhile the indigenous Merriam's subspecies of elk went extinct, and the Rocky Mountain subspecies was also extirpated.

Barker was involved in getting Smokey Bear (see chapter 16) recognized as a fire-prevention symbol. He and his younger brother,

Elliott Barker in 1946. Center for Southwest Research Digital Collections, 182934. Photo by Harold D. Walter.

S. Omar Barker, the western writer and poet, represent the best of early American New Mexico. And, to him, Beattys Cabin was the heart of the wilderness he loved.

Hiking to Beattys Cabin is the quintessential Pecos Wilderness experience. Two routes exist. They're about equal in distance (5 to 6 miles one way), and both are moderately strenuous. Both traverse long mesas through high mountain meadows with breathtaking views.

Until recently I always approached Beattys Cabin from Hamilton Mesa, among my favorite Pecos hikes. The views of the entire region from the open meadows on the mesa are staggering, the trail is easy, and the high-country wildflowers, especially the wild iris, alone are worth the trip. The Hamilton Mesa route begins at Iron Gate Campground, reached by a dirt road that can be steep

CHAPTER THREE

and rough and very difficult when wet. After little more than half a mile, the trail splits, the eastern fork slanting downhill to Mora Flats on the Rio Mora, a popular day-hiking and camping destination. The western fork goes northeast to ascend Hamilton Mesa, where at about 1.75 miles from Iron Gate it leaves the forest for the mesa's open meadows. Here, the vastness of the Pecos Wilderness is spread before you. At 3.7 miles from Iron Gate, at N 35 53 08 / W 105 35 34, is the junction with the trail slabbing downhill north-northwest through forest to Beattys Cabin, while the other trail goes north-northeast to Pecos Falls.

The other route to Beattys Cabin is from Jacks Creek Campground near Cowles. The trail ascends steeply and steadily until at about two miles it goes around the south side of Round Mountain, traversing meadows with good views as well as stands of aspens. The trail peaks at around three to four miles before beginning its descent to the valley of the Pecos River. The total one-way distance is slightly more than six miles.

The meadows around Beattys Cabin are closed to camping.

For those who, like me, enjoy GPS, the Rio Sebadilloses and the Pecos River come together at Beattys Cabin at N 35 54 30.5 / W 105 35 48.

Hiking Considerations

Cattle still graze in the Pecos Wilderness as they have for centuries, allowed as a prior traditional use. That means cows and cow droppings. Once, while my family and I were camped on Hamilton Mesa, a cow herd wandered through our camp in the middle of the night, making a mess of everything.

Also, many people still travel the Pecos Wilderness as Barker did, with pack animals: horses, mules, and sometimes llamas. These animals also can make a mess of the trails. Try to keep a good historic perspective.

To that end, consider this: not until the mid-twentieth century were backpacks used at all in the Pecos backcountry. Travel in the wilderness was by horses or mules. In 1948 two young men attempted something novel: they would spend two weeks camping and fishing in the wilderness *on foot!* Their backpacking was so unusual that *New Mexico Magazine* ran a feature article about the trip. By 1960 backpackers outnumbered horse riders in the wilderness.

But while portions of the Pecos Wilderness receive very heavy use, other areas are seldom visited; 85 percent of hikers use 15 percent of the trails. I recall a trip to Pecos Falls, at the height of the summer hiking season, during which my buddy and I spent a day hiking the headwaters of the Pecos River—and didn't encounter another hiker. The most frequently traveled trails are those leading to Beattys Cabin, Pecos Falls, Puerto Nambe, the Truchas and other high peaks, and the lake basins. But after Labor Day, visitation even of these areas declines precipitously, and early fall in the Pecos is magnificent.

Down in the flat, I look for signs of the original Beattys Cabin (which are negligible). This would have indeed been a perfect site for a cabin (or a "ranch," as Beatty would have it). For that reason, and by habit, I look for artifacts, bits of nonlocal stone. Any early Native people would have been attracted to this place. I look for the stumps of trees logged long ago.

Then it's time to leave. Regrettably, this was a day hike, not a backpacking trip. And regrettably I'm not ten years old. I've spent a lot of time in wild nature since those expeditions to Heart Lake. But some features are permanent. As I hike, a breeze ruffles the fir branches; the air is cool and clean; I can smell the forest; there is no human-made sound; and the wilderness is as wild as ever.

Most references to this area spell it "Beatty's Cabin," with the possessive apostrophe, but the US Board on Geographic Names (USBGN), at their first board meeting in 1891, established a policy whereby the names of geographic features in the United States

CHAPTER THREE

would not use the possessive apostrophe, and the policy has persisted despite criticism.

I follow the USBGN's policies, and so does the State Names Committee (which I have chaired), so I feel bound to use the names precisely as spelled in the US Geographic Names Information System (GNIS) database, which is a compilation of all the US place names that have been recorded so far (a lot). Also, by federal statute, these names and only these are approved for use in federal maps and publications. With respect to the topic of this chapter, I could be perfectly safe and call it by its GNIS name: Beatty Cabin.

But that name seems just plain awkward and ugly, and I've never heard anyone use it, most people keeping the possessive 's. Local usage is the ultimate arbiter with names. So I compromised: I used "Beattys Cabin"—keeping the local pronunciation but with the USBGN spelling. *Nothing* about names is ever simple.

CHAPTER FOUR

New Mexico's Hermit

SOMETIMES ONLY A thin line separates religiosity from insanity. Consider the Hermit of Hermit Peak.

I pondered that as my hiking partner, David Ryan, and his three adventure dogs—Teddy, Paddy, and Petey—began slogging up the steep, brutally rough trail to the wilderness cave where the Hermit had lived for five years: on top of 10,259-foot Hermit Peak in the Pecos Wilderness. How had he even found this place? After all, promoting residential cave property atop a remote mountain wasn't exactly a high priority for the Las Vegas (New Mexico) Chamber of Commerce in the 1860s.

And as David, dogs, and I plodded upward on a trail that seemed strewn with every loose rock on the mountain, I also wondered about the pilgrims who had visited him and brought him food and supplies. Most of them used horses, mules, or donkeys, but even then it would have been a difficult journey. It occurred to me that if someone was seeking to atone for sins, this certainly would be an effective penance. If I had to hike this trail every time I sinned, I'd

CHAPTER FOUR

think twice about sinning. No wonder local people regarded the Hermit as a holy man.

The story of Juan Maria de Agostini, the eponymous Hermit of Hermit Peak and also of Hermit Cave in the foothills of the Organ Mountains east of Las Cruces, is well-known in New Mexican folklore, but it's worth retelling. Born into Italian nobility in Novara around 1800, he was well educated, multilingual, and widely read. Agostini (or Agostiniani or Mateo Baccalini or Giovanni Marsa de Agostini; variants of his name are numerous) may have studied for the priesthood—he was known as Padre Matteo, for Matthew, his patron saint—but rather than becoming a priest he took to wandering. Legend says that he fought with Garibaldi in the campaign for Italian unification and fled Italy under curse by the pope, although another story says that he left because of a failed love affair. Allegedly, he made clear that his austere life was penance for some terrible crime he had committed. All these stories are apocryphal.

He wandered throughout Europe, South America, Mexico, Cuba, and Canada, living as a hermit and ministering to the poor wherever he went. At some point he left Canada for the United States; in 1859 he had a photographic portrait made in New York City. Then he headed west.

The year 1862 (or 1863) found him living in a rock shelter near Council Grove, Kansas, on the Santa Fe Trail. Bearing a letter of recommendation from several citizens of Saint Louis, he approached Eugenio Romero, a merchant and contractor, about joining his wagon train returning to New Mexico, insisting that he walk the 550 miles rather than ride.

In response to Agostini's request for a cave to live in, Romero took him to Romeroville, just south of Las Vegas, where there was a cave by a creek, but he stayed only a few months before moving to the cave on Cerro del Tecolote ("Peak of the Owl"), now better known as Hermit Peak. In that cave, and in three crude, wooden huts built for him by his followers, he lived. He obtained food from

Juan Maria de Agostini, aka the Hermit. Photo courtesy of the New Mexico State University Archives.

visitors and water from a spring that became known as Hermit Spring, which still exists (N 35 44 43 / W 105 25 13.5).

The trail we hiked had become steeper and rockier the higher we went, and we were relieved to finally reach the mountain's relatively flat top. Hermit Spring was dry.

We strode across the mesa to its southern edge (N 35 44 39 / W 105 24 48.5). There, we beheld a view that on a clear day might stretch to Texas. Did the Hermit come here to sit in meditation, to watch the daily panorama, the progression of the seasons, the aspens bright green in the spring, gold in the fall, the plains' subtle changes? Did he come here at night to behold the heavens, revealed with almost miraculous vividness and clarity? If he wanted to experience the overarching grandeur of God as manifested in nature, this would be a good place to do it.

CHAPTER FOUR

Devotional offering in the Hermit's cave. Photo by David Ryan.

But David and I wanted to see where he likely spent most of his time—in his cave. We followed a steep, rough trail, unmarked except for crude tree-branch crucifixes—stations of the Cross—down to the cave (N 35 44 31 / W 105 24 56).

Actually, it's more of an overhang than a cave. The ceiling has been blackened by smoke from countless fires. Pilgrims have placed crosses and shrines in niches in the rocks; on a previous visit, I found offerings and votive candles burning. Low rock walls formed a crude vestibule. It was not exactly a room with a view, as trees blocked the nearby cliffs, although a short scramble leads to a breathtaking view of Hermit Peak's vertical face; no place for anyone with vertigo. A visitor described a visit to the Hermit on a cold, wet day in May 1866:

> His age does not go below sixty-five years. He is of small stature; plump and well-proportioned body; fair complexion; blue eyes; long and graying, venerable beard; a somber and

imposing expression commanding respect from all who see him; instructive conversation; devout countenance; and a hospitable and frank nature which makes him amiable, as he shares his frugal nutrients with whomever visits him. He himself is always willing to prepare a corn meal gruel with water and salt, clean and well-cooked; his table is a rock slab loosened from the same crevice and is well situated under the porch of his small cabin. Courteous without ceremony, he invites his guests without formality or commotion.

This rare man involves himself in a mysterious life, which causes some persons to form rash impressions, others compassionate ones, and finally, all to preoccupy themselves with the hermit and his life of solitude. His exercise consists of meditation and prayer; he begs from no one, nor does he visit anybody, but he will accept invitations with modest courtesy, and as in our case, they serve a purpose, such as to cure a sick person, instruct a family, or carry out some other pious duty, on which type of visits he rarely sits; he works to furnish his sustenance. He is very much given to study.

Personally, I found the "cave" dark, cramped, and more than a little gloomy; I'm just not good hermit material. It would have been cold and drafty in winter. I heard that the Hermit actually had another cave, a real one, where he lived, reserving this one for receiving visitors. Did pilgrims come even in winter, over a trail that would have been all but impassable? A few must have, at least when the trail was open, bringing supplies and receiving in return healing, blessing, and sometimes little hand-carved religious artifacts. He became a local saint; in Las Vegas his devotees formed the Sociedad del Ermitaño, and at Easter people there still make rosaries of native plants in his memory. As the offerings in the cave testify, they still visit where he lived.

For five years he lived atop the peak—then he departed. With the same opacity of motive that led him up the mountain, he came down.

CHAPTER FOUR

He went south. In 1867 he accompanied the wagon train of don Ramón González to the lower Mesilla Valley to consult a lawyer, Colonel Albert J. Fountain, on a legal matter; then he walked to San Antonio, Texas, and later to a cave near Juárez, Mexico.

In 1869 he often visited the Barela family on the plaza in Mesilla, sometimes preaching in their home. He told the Barelas of his plans to live in La Cueva.

It was an appealing choice. La Cueva is a natural cave situated in a volcanic rhyolitic ashfall tuff formation in the western foothills of the Organ Mountains. It's shallow but still more sheltered than the Cerro del Tecolote cave. Several springs and even an occasionally flowing stream are nearby, along with a rich assortment of native plants that the Hermit could use in his healing. Archaeologists have determined that people have used the cave and its resources for at least five thousand years.

When I hiked the easy 0.65-mile La Cueva Trail from the picnic area at the Bureau of Land Management's A. B. Cox Outdoor Recreation Area, I noted the plants I encountered: scrub oak, squaw bush, juniper, ephedra, several kinds of yucca and mesquite, barrel cactus, aloysia, sotol, fourwing saltbush, willows, dodder. The Hermit would have known many, many more.

One of Agostini's devotees, Antonio García, kindly transported suffering people to La Cueva for treatment by the Hermit. Today it's an easy ten-mile drive from University Boulevard at the south end of Las Cruces, but then it would have been a long, rough ride—and in the 1860s, a dangerous one.

The Barela family warned El Ermitaño against living alone in such a remote place. His response was typical of the man of faith: "I shall make a fire in front of my cave every Friday evening, and if you see it I shall be alive. If the fire fails to appear, it will be because I have been killed. I shall bless you daily in my prayers."

One Friday night in the spring of 1869, the fire failed to appear. Antonio García led a posse to the cave to find the hermit lying face down on his crucifix, a knife in his back. He was wearing a penitential girdle full of spikes.

The Hermit's cave in the Organ Mountains, located at the base of this formation. Photo by Robert Julyan.

El Ermitaño is buried in the Mesilla cemetery. The gravestone reads, in Spanish: "Juan Maria Justiniano, Hermit of the Old and New World. He died on the 17th of April 1869 at 69 years and 49 years a hermit." His murder was one of many unsolved murders in the late 1800s in Doña Ana County.

Of all the New Mexicans I have read and written about—outlaws, Indian warriors, soldiers, civic leaders, scientists—El Ermitaño remains the one I most would like to have met, for he was the rarest of all: a man of profound complexities but also of genuine goodwill and peace.

CHAPTER FIVE

Jaramillo Creek
Where Plate Tectonics Came Together

THE VALLES CALDERA, literally the heart of the Jemez Mountains, is magnificent in its vastness and beauty—breathtaking, chatoyant grasslands upon which graze majestic elk, surrounded by domed mountains exceeding eleven thousand feet, born in volcanic eruptions dwarfing that of Mount Saint Helens in Washington. This spectacular scenery is worthy of a national park, which someday it might become: it is New Mexico nature at its grandest.

Thus it's ironic that among the Valles Caldera's most significant features are little holes, each only about the size of a half-dollar in diameter and a little more than six inches deep, drilled by geoscientists in the 1960s into the scattered lava formations. Profoundly significant on a global scale, the age and paleomagnetic measurements of those cores proved conclusively the theory of plate tectonics and proved as well that the earth's surface is composed of continent-sized plates, whose slow but inexorable movements are responsible for almost all of the planet's large-scale features—and many smaller ones—from the Himalayan Mountains to the shape of the oceans, from the Red Sea to the Great Rift Valley in Africa,

CHAPTER FIVE

A hole drilled by geophysicists in volcanic rock in the Jemez Mountains, by the roadside on NM 4. Photo by Robert Julyan.

from the deepest of the deep-sea trenches to the earth's most explosive volcanoes and most destructive earthquakes. These shifting plates have been partly responsible in New Mexico for most of the state's topography, from the valley of the Rio Grande Rift to many of New Mexico's mountains.

A significant theory indeed.

Development of the theory of plate tectonics (the word "theory" doesn't mean that it's not a proven fact but rather that it's a comprehensive explanation) is among humankind's greatest scientific and intellectual achievements. And the final piece of this grand picture was found in the Valles Caldera, in these inconspicuous little drill holes.

They are so inconspicuous, in fact, that until recently the resource managers at the Valles Caldera didn't know their locations. Sure, the scientists in the 1960s recorded where they drilled, but those geographic coordinates weren't as precise as they would be today with global positioning technology; the text descriptions the geologists wrote were often ambiguous; and the holes subsequently could have been obscured by dirt and vegetation. The holes were largely ignored and forgotten.

Until 2007, that is, when biologist Robert Parmenter suggested to the Valles Caldera National Preserve that finding the holes and documenting them would be a good project for volunteers. Ana Steffen, archaeologist and cultural resources coordinator at the Valles Caldera National Preserve, agreed. She also wanted to protect and showcase this important part of the Valles Caldera's history, so she turned to a man and a woman retired from the Los Alamos National Laboratory, Tom Lyttle, a geochemist, and Donna Smith, an economic geologist.

And it is with them that I am sitting in the Valles Caldera National Preserve's offices in Jemez Springs, talking about their quest to locate and document the holes associated with what geoscientists have come to know as the Jaramillo Paleomagnetic Event.

But first, a little about geomagnetism. Anyone who's used a compass knows that the earth acts as a magnet, just like an iron bar magnet, with one end of the needle pointing toward the North Pole. That's because the earth has a liquid iron core and spins on an axis. Our planet is unique among the solar system's planets in having a magnetic field. That's why we can use compasses here but not on Mercury or Mars.

What was not known until the mid-1900s is that this field occasionally reverses polarity; during a reversal, the north needle of a compass points south. During the past million years, the earth's polarity has reversed at least twice. What's more, magnetic minerals in rocks keep a record of the polarity that existed when the rocks crystallized out of molten rock called *magma*. Thus geoscientists can ascertain the earth's magnetic polarity at the time the rocks formed. They have given names to these periods of normal and reversed polarity; we currently are living during the Brunhes normal (our compass needles point north) polarity epoch, which has lasted about eight hundred thousand years. Geologists call each reversal an *event*. As New Mexico geoscientist Fraser Goff has explained, these reversals occur because the molten part of the core moves, or convects, due to the earth's rotation. The core is nickel-iron, and when a magnetic substance moves it generates a magnetic field. When the movement's direction abruptly changes, the polarity changes.

CHAPTER FIVE

During the 1950s and 1960s geoscientists studying seafloor spreading on both sides of huge, linear mid-ocean cracks had difficulty explaining what appeared to be bands of alternating normal and reversed polarity on seafloor basalt. As Goff summarized, "Finally, some researchers theorized that each stripe represented basalt erupted during different magnetic polarity time periods. But where to prove this? If reversals were recorded in the ocean, certainly there should be a place on land to verify the process."

Enter the Valles Caldera. In the 1960s geologist Robert Smith was working in the caldera, trying to date the Bandelier Tuff and postcaldera domes that rose after the main eruptions. While in Hawaii at a conference he met geoscientists Brent Dalrymple and Richard Doell, who were working on dating paleomagnetic events. They needed a site on land where deposition had been constant. Smith suggested the volcanic domes of rhyolite in the Valles Caldera. Intrigued, Dalrymple and Doell proposed that if they drilled in the Valles Caldera, they would give Smith the dates he needed. They went to New Mexico and began drilling, at nineteen places in all, sixteen in the Valles Caldera itself.

They found that the magnetic polarity pattern and ages of the rhyolite domes matched the polarities and ages of the ocean-floor basalts, showing a connection between the presumed movement of the continents and what was happening on the ocean floor. The continents were the expression of plates driven by upwellings in the seafloor. It was a "Eureka!" moment. As Goff explained in his book *Valles Caldera: A Geologic History*, "Because the alternating ages and magnetic polarities of the caldera can be correlated with ages and polarities of young basalts erupted on the seafloor, the early paleomagnetic results in the valleys are considered pivotal to the general acceptance of plate tectonics."

Today, plate tectonics is universally accepted. In fact, it is as central to the earth sciences as the theory of evolution is to biology and as Copernicus's theory that the earth revolves around the sun is to astronomy. But one hundred years ago the idea of continent-sized plates of the planet's crust floating around on the hot, plastic

The Valles Caldera in the Jemez Mountains, with a volcanic resurgent dome in the left-center. Photo by Robert Julyan.

mantle was just plain bizarre, even though it explained troublesome geological mysteries such as earthquakes and volcanoes and why the coasts of Africa and South America look like they would fit together like jigsaw puzzle pieces. A good theory, but it took small drill cores from the Valles Caldera to prove it completely.

But those holes could not have been drilled in just any rocks. It took the Jemez Mountains' geologic history to confirm the earth's geologic history. And both involve the outpouring of magma from deep below the surface.

In north-central New Mexico two great volcanic eruptions occurred 1.62 and 1.25 million years ago, spewing immense pyroclastic flows and ash, hundreds of feet thick, over a wide area to create the present Jemez Mountains and Pajarito Plateau, forming multicolored geologic formations found in Valles Caldera National Preserve, Bandelier National Monument, Kasha-Katuwe Tent Rocks National Monument, and Battleship Rock State Park. Also

CHAPTER FIVE

created then were several obsidian deposits used by Native peoples throughout the Southwest, and springs heated by residual heat retained far below the surface.

The major eruptions, however, were only the precursor to the Valles Caldera. When the eruptions ceased and the magma chamber was depleted of gas and magma, the roof of the magma chamber collapsed on itself, forming a caldera. Then the remaining gas and magma surged upward from beneath the caldera, uplifting the central floor to form the resurgent dome of Redondo Peak. Finally, the continued rise of magma around the perimeter of the resurgent dome created rhyolite domes such as Cerro del Medio, Cerro del Abrigo, and others like a moat around the caldera. Today these various volcanic features form the high peaks of the Jemez Mountains: San Antonio Mountain, 9,978 feet; Cerro Toledo, 10,825 feet; Polvadera Peak, 11,232 feet; and Redondo Peak, 11,254 feet. The range's highest point, Chicoma Mountain, 11,562 feet, is a precaldera volcanic dome.

It was the resurgence and eruption of postcaldera domes that led in circuitous fashion to the drill holes. These rhyolite domes emerged at different ages, and therefore the magnetic polarity in their rocks should correspond to the earth's polarity at the time they erupted. And indeed they do: Cerro del Abrigo, one million years old, is normally polarized; Cerro Santa Rosa (0.94 million years old) is transitionally polarized; and Cerro Seco and Cerro San Luis, both 0.8 million years old, and Cerro Santa Rosa II, 0.79 million years old, are all reverse polarized. Later rhyolite domes, such as San Antonio Mountain (0.55 million years old), are normally polarized. And they all match up with the pattern of magnetic polarities of the midocean ridges. Plate tectonics confirmed.

Because Cerro del Abrigo at the beginning of the sequence is located just south of Jaramillo Creek in the Valles Caldera, the subsequent polarization was called the Jaramillo Paleomagnetic Event. Mention the Jaramillo Event to geoscientists and they might bow their heads in reverence.

But after the holes were drilled, the cores taken, the results analyzed, the major scientific papers written, and the conclusions drawn, the little holes were largely forgotten.

For Lyttle and Smith, rediscovering the drill holes is a genuine labor of love. For one thing, it has allowed them access to the Valles Caldera and its spectacular natural history. "The elk can be a bit of a distraction in looking for the holes," says Lyttle ironically.

Smith says that the two have also encountered deer, turkeys, lynx, and coyotes.

Their work has also required them to be detectives. The old project descriptions can get them in the general area of the holes, but finding the actual holes requires drill-hole forensics. "The drilling would have been done by Doell and his graduate students carrying heavy drilling equipment and water—thirty to forty gallons—so they would try to drill at sites as close to their vehicle as possible," says Lyttle.

Also, Doell and the students were aided by Robert Smith and Roy Bailey, who were looking for vertical flow features in the rhyolitic lava in which to drill.

"The holes are round and sharp," says Smith, "and the human eye is pretty good at picking up patterns."

Relying on text descriptions in the original report, including geographic coordinates not up to modern standards of precision, they have been able to find three to four drill-hole locations each year. As of summer 2013 they had about five yet to discover.

At present, roaming around the Valles Caldera by oneself is not permitted, but Steffen says that once the inventory is completed, access points and trails will be created. Almost all the drill holes require hiking.

Lyttle and Smith directed me to two drill-hole sites not in the national preserve. One was on a road cut in South Mountain rhyolite, immediately west of where NM 4 crosses the east fork of the Jemez River. The coordinates for this site are N 35 49 41 / W 106 35 29. Just watch for traffic if looking for these.

But the other set of holes, they said, was atop the volcanic

CHAPTER FIVE

formation called Battleship Rock. I made the tough, steep scramble to the top and began searching for the holes, but despite the area being relatively exposed and well defined, I couldn't find them. Discouraged, I began descending by a different route than I had come up. And suddenly there they were. Not on Battleship's top but on its sides, two clusters of the holes. If you wish to see them, here are the coordinates: N 35 49 40.3 / W 106 38 23.3. But no clearly defined trail leads to them, and the uphill scramble is very steep and difficult. How the geologists got the drills and water there is beyond me.

Geologists, like archaeologists and other scientists, are famous for eliciting large-scale information of enormous significance from small pieces of evidence. I can't say that I felt our earth shift beneath me when I gazed at the holes, but if someone else does, I might believe them.

To Learn More

Read *Valles Caldera: A Geologic History*, by Fraser Goff (Albuquerque: University of New Mexico Press, 2009). With colorful charts and diagrams, lots of color photos, and clear, concise text, this is a superb introduction to the geology of the Valles Caldera, including information about geomagnetism and the Jaramillo Paleomagnetic Event.

Read *The Road to Jaramillo: Critical Years of the Revolution in Earth Science*, by William Glen (Stanford, CA: Stanford University Press, 1982). This is the definitive book about plate tectonics and the Jaramillo Event, but it's difficult to obtain and pretty heavy going for nonspecialists.

Visit the Valles Caldera National Preserve visitors' center in Jemez Springs and ask about the status of the drill-hole project. Public access and interpretative materials may be available by the time this book is published.

CHAPTER SIX

The Battle of Glorieta Pass

HISTORIANS OF THE Civil War call the Battle of Glorieta Pass "the Gettysburg of the West." Indeed it was, for just as Gettysburg halted the Confederate invasion of Union territory in the North, so the March 1862 battle in New Mexico terminated what had been a successful Confederate invasion of Union territory in the West, crushing their hopes here. And it all hinged upon a bold march across Glorieta Mesa.

Like Robert E. Lee's march into Pennsylvania, the Confederate invasion of northern New Mexico began well. In 1862 southern New Mexico and Arizona were Confederate territory and jointly administered as the Territory of Arizona. The strategy was to send an invasion force north from the territory's capital at Mesilla to seize the rest of New Mexico en route to Colorado with its rich gold and silver assets, before moving on to California and its mines and seaports. The force was led by Brigadier General Henry Hopkins Sibley. In early 1862 Sibley led his soldiers, mostly Texans, north along the Rio Grande.

He was opposed by Union forces under Colonel Edward Canby,

CHAPTER SIX

Major John Chivington. Courtesy of the Center for Southwest Research Digital Collections.

and they met first near Fort Craig. At the Battle of Valverde, the Union forces were forced to retreat to the fort, while the Confederates continued north. They captured Albuquerque, then Santa Fe. They were poised to enter Glorieta Pass via the Santa Fe Trail and proceed onto the plains for the capture of Fort Union, the major Union stronghold and supply point on the route north.

The Confederates, led by Charles L. Pyron and William Read Scurry, were a strong force of soldiers and artillery. They knew they faced an equally formidable force led by Colonel John P. Slough of the First Colorado Infantry, with units commanded by Major John M. Chivington. On March 26, 1862, the battle was joined.

On the first day, the troops skirmished and maneuvered to no definite conclusion. A charge led by Chivington captured Confederate cannons and boosted Union morale.

The second day, the troops recuperated and tended to the dead and wounded. Reinforcements arrived for both sides.

On the third day, March 28, the battle was fought in earnest.

THE BATTLE OF GLORIETA PASS

Slough's plan included Chivington attacking the Confederate flanks from the slopes of Glorieta Mesa on the south side of the pass.

It is Saturday, March 20, 2013, a warm, dry, spring day, and my hiking partner, David Ryan, and I are retracing the route over which Major John Chivington led 530 federal officers and troops, mostly the Colorado Volunteers, up onto Glorieta Mesa. Much has changed during the exactly 151 years and 2 days since Union soldiers made the same trip. For one thing, it was cold and snowy when the Union officers led their men across the mesa, whereas it was borderline hot and dry when we went. Moreover, they were leading soldiers, whereas we were leading three dogs—Teddy, Paddy, and Petey. And the biggest difference is that we cheated. The Union troops started from Kozlowski's Ranch on the Santa Fe Trail and marched up what was called Cristobal Canyon and the Galisteo Road to the mesa's top, whereas we drove David's vehicle up the canyon over what is now called the La Joya Road / Forest Road 612.

On the mesa's top, the soldiers likely would have rested briefly from their ascent before moving on. We parked our car and mustered the dogs before proceeding. Almost immediately we faced an obstacle the soldiers would not have faced: a formidable herd of large Charolais cows near a muddy water hole. Resolutely, we marched around them. Then we faced another difficulty: I got us lost. The historian Jerry Thompson had sketched on a Forest Service map the route Chivington took, and I had plotted that on a topographic map along with GPS way points, but nonetheless I discovered that we were going astray amid the spaghetti bowl of roads, wheel ruts, and cow paths, with no landmarks to guide us. A cross-country hike finally put us back on course.

Chivington would have faced similar bewilderment, made even worse by dense thickets of piñon, juniper, ponderosas, and Gambel oak, the few trails obscured by snow. Moreover, the Colorado Volunteers he led had no knowledge of the local terrain. Fortunately, they were guided by Lieutenant Colonel Manuel Chaves and his contingent of volunteers, the Second New Mexico Infantry. Twenty

CHAPTER SIX

years earlier Chaves had been with New Mexico governor Manuel Armijo when Mexican troops confronted another force of invading Texans, defeating and imprisoning them. When in 1847 Governor Armijo faced a much stronger force of invaders, US troops under General Stephen Watts Kearny at Apache Canyon, Chaves had argued for a more robust defense, but Armijo had ignored him and withdrawn. Chaves had scouted the area then and later run a large sheep operation in the Pecos area. A few days before the Battle of Glorieta Pass he'd already proven his bravery against Confederates by leading a daring raid against Santa Fe.

Moreover, Chaves had with him as lead scout one Anastasio Duran, a resident of the Hispanic village of Chaperito who was stationed at Fort Union. Described as a Comanchero by US Army officers, someone who ventured onto the eastern foothills and plains to trade with the Comanches, Duran was well-known for his hunting skills. He knew Glorieta Mesa thoroughly.

It was likely while Chivington and his troops were resting atop Glorieta Mesa that a decision was made that was to have far-reaching—and controversial—consequences.

Chivington's orders had been to position himself for a flank attack in support of Slough's Colorado Volunteers in Glorieta Pass. But while the Union troops were on the mesa, Chaves's scouts reported seeing the Confederate supply camp at Johnson's Ranch in Apache Canyon, at the rear of the battlefield—and lightly defended. It has been reported that the debate over whether to ignore Slough's orders and instead capture the supply wagons took over an hour before the decision was made. And in fact some historians have argued that it was not Chivington but rather a prominent Bureau of Indian Affairs agent, James L. Collins, who suggested the change of plans. Collins, a newspaperman, was later praised by Chivington as a "brave man" and invaluable as a guide and interpreter. Finding the supply wagons was a lucky accident.

The Union troops made their way down the steep slopes of the mesa, surprised the Confederates, and, after a brief battle with relatively few casualties on both sides, burned eighty supply wagons,

THE BATTLE OF GLORIETA PASS

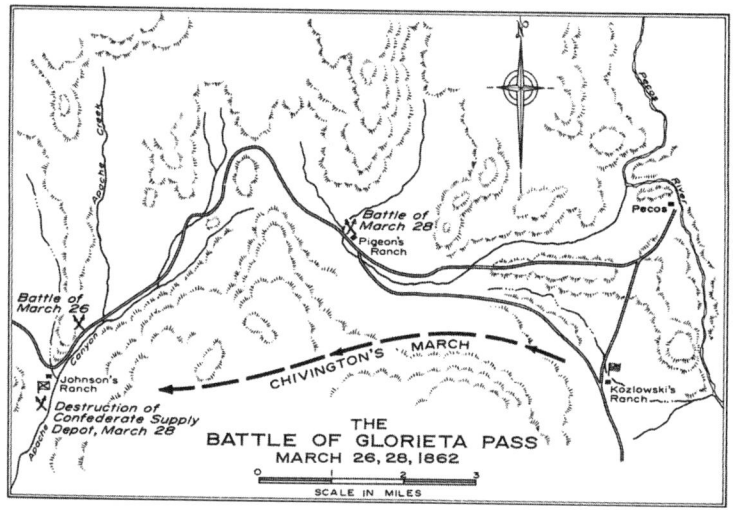

Map of the Battle of Glorieta Pass. Courtesy of the National Park Service.

spiked several cannons, and killed or drove off five hundred horses and mules.

In the meantime, in Glorieta Pass a furious and bloody battle raged between the two sides, and when darkness fell Slough was forced to make a tactical retreat.

After the battle, many people charged that had Chivington obeyed his orders and supported the main body of troops, the Union forces would have been victorious instead of having to retreat. Chivington's forces made up approximately one-third of the Union total.

David and I and the dogs faced no such indecision. Like the soldiers, we marched over the rolling pastures and forested hills to the mesa's brink.

According to Thompson, Chivington's forces followed a faint game trail northwest. David and I faced more roads and tracks and trails than there are highways in downtown LA. For obvious reasons, the soldiers didn't record what they saw as they marched. David and I could afford to be a little more observant.

CHAPTER SIX

The cliffs of Glorieta Mesa. Photo by Robert Julyan.

We saw two flocks of wild turkeys. Surely deer and elk would be abundant, for despite its current hard use by local people the mesa is still a superb game habitat.

Because David and I (and the dogs) usually are doing archaeological inventories together, we focused on the ground perhaps more than we should have, but we quickly noticed "lithics"—nonlocal stones that have been flaked or chipped or rubbed or otherwise altered by humans. Certainly the Towa-speaking Indians of nearby Pecos Pueblo would have hunted here. And when a midsection we found later was said to possibly be Paleo-Indian in origin (approximately eleven thousand to eight thousand years ago), it reminded us that humans were hunting on this mesa when the people who later built the Egyptian pyramids lived in grass huts.

At the mesa's brink we found not a rough trail as we expected but rather a wide road created by a bulldozer for an unknown purpose. Expecting that it would lead into Apache Canyon and the site of Johnson's Ranch, near which the Confederates were billeted, we followed it downward. Despite having once been bladed smooth, the road was now badly eroded and very steep. Nonetheless, it was infinitely preferable to going straight downhill through the forest, as I imagined the soldiers doing. At one point we saw a very old track heading straight downhill, clogged with rocks and clearly not having been used in a long time. Could this have been the route followed by the soldiers? For by now I was convinced that the troops' guides must have led them to a track or road or path; they could not have simply plunged down the mesa's cliff-like slopes. The losses would have been enormous.

We continued down the road until it split. We chose the most likely direction and followed it until it abruptly ended at concrete buttresses over a gully and a very narrow, rough trail sloping downward. By this time we concluded we'd achieved our goal, more or less; my GPS unit said that Johnson's Ranch was less than a third of a mile away.

Later, from the National Park Service guide at Pecos National Monument, which has developed a hiking trail through the battlefield, I learned that our decision was probably wise. While no one knows for sure which route off the mesa the Union forces took, likely it was via a drainage south of the one we took.

The National Park Service guide knew exactly where the Confederate supply wagons had been, in the flats just south of Johnson's Ranch, and they had a pretty good idea which draw Chivington had descended, down a steep draw two-thirds of a mile south of Johnson's Ranch to enter just east of the present Cañoncito Siding. The hike from Kozlowski's Ranch to the mesa's rim was nine miles. Jerry Thompson has given a good description of what Chivington would have seen when he cautiously looked down:

> Five hundred feet below the rim of the canyon, as many as 200 disorganized and indefensible Rebels, cooks, teamsters, convalescents, hospital stewards, and a few guards, all casually milling about. Some of the Texans were even running foot races. . . . Below in plain view was Scurry's entire supply train and as many as 500 horses and mules, either tethered or in a corral at the base of the mesa.

All previous doubts vanished. The prize was irresistible. Chivington ordered his men to proceed down the slope.

CHAPTER SIX

The story of the capture and destruction of the supply wagons is well-known. Food, blankets, ammunition, medical supplies, everything the Confederate troops depended upon—all burned, destroyed. Hundreds of horses and mules. What the Union troops did with them is still debated. Did the soldiers, as some have charged, bayonet them? Chivington himself boasted of killing 1,100. But then almost all his bombastic claims were false or exaggerated, and other historians have said that the animals likely were turned loose and swelled the herds of the local people.

Then Chivington, fearing that the main Confederate force would suddenly appear from up the narrow canyon, ordered his men to climb back up the steep escarpment and back onto the mesa top. There they were met by Lieutenant Alfred S. Cobb, who told him that the main federal force, after fierce fighting around Pigeon's Ranch, had retreated to Kozlowski's Ranch. That meant that Chivington could not return via the canyon he had ascended.

Thompson, whose map guided our adventure, vividly tells the story of the almost miraculous arrival of Alexander Grzelachowski, local merchant, innkeeper, and former priest. "I know a route," Grzelachowski proclaimed from atop a magnificent white horse. He then guided them through a snowstorm to Kozlowki's Ranch, where they announced their conquest to their dispirited fellow soldiers. Soon after arrival, the wonderful white horse dropped dead of exhaustion.

At the time, confusion certainly existed among the federals as to what actually had been achieved, but the Confederates certainly knew. Ten days later they began their long retreat from New Mexico. They had entered New Mexico with hundreds of wagons—and returned with three. For the Confederacy, it was all over in the West.

After the battle Captain A. W. Evans would write, "The services of Lt. Col. Manuel Chaves in the affair at Apache Canyon were of the most valuable character to the Union." Chivington himself, however, ignored the contributions of New Mexicans in recommending promotions and rewards. Despite being the so-called Hero of Glorieta Pass, Chivington was widely disliked.

Chivington's reputation was permanently stained less than two years later, when in November 1864 he led the Colorado Volunteers in a massacre, accompanied by depraved atrocities and mutilations, of peaceful Arapaho and Cheyenne Indians—mostly the elderly, women, and children—camped on Sand Creek in Colorado. The appalling massacre shocked the nation. Several inquiries were made, which resulted in Sand Creek forever being a blotch on America's history and preventing Chivington from being remembered as the Hero of Glorieta. Instead the label most often attached to his name is the one scrawled at a Battle of Glorieta Pass folk-art memorial on Interstate 25 east of the battle site: "Baby Killer."

To Learn More

Visit the Pecos National Monument visitors' center, talk to the staff, take a tour of the battlefield, and hike the self-guided battlefield trail. And while you're there, visit the ruins of Pecos Pueblo and the mission the Spaniards established there.

Read Jerry Thompson's book about the Civil War campaign in the West, *A Civil War History of the New Mexico Volunteers and Militia* (Albuquerque: University of New Mexico Press, 2015).

CHAPTER SEVEN

La Bajada

Every Automobile's Worst Nightmare

TODAY THE OLD road up La Bajada (the Descent) is quiet, peaceful, like a battlefield long after the guns have been silenced, but if you close your eyes and open your imagination you can hear the tormented cries of drivers and vehicles from long ago: the keening of dying transmissions, hisses of steam escaping from overheated radiators, the screeches of tortured brake pads, the curses of angry, frustrated drivers. This is all even easier to imagine if you stumble on the steep, rocky grade or stub your toe on a sharp lava rock.

Even on foot you can be inspired to curse La Bajada.

No one knows for sure when the old La Bajada road acquired its notoriety as possibly the gnarliest half mile in New Mexico. And accentuating that notoriety is the contrast with the present Interstate 25 route about 2.5 miles to the northeast—straight, smooth as butter, barely requiring a single downshift to make it up the six-hundred-foot escarpment.

So distinct a boundary are these cliffs that in Spanish colonial times this escarpment delineated the province's two administrative

CHAPTER SEVEN

regions: the Rio Arriba "up river" and the Rio Abajo "down river." Subtle cultural differences from that era persist to this day, including the name of a northern county.

Dr. Joseph Sanchez, director of the National Park Service's Spanish Colonial Research Center at the University of New Mexico, once told me that while La Bajada certainly would have been familiar to travelers on the old Spanish route between Santa Fe and Chihuahua—a historic marker calls it "the most difficult of the obstacles on the Camino Real"—they mentioned it neither in their journals nor on their maps.

Actually, Sanchez points out, the Camino Real was not one trail but a network of routes, and most travelers, especially those with wagons, approached Santa Fe via Galisteo and the Rio Galisteo. Others, he said, followed the Santa Fe River to La Cienega.

The explorer Zebulon Pike, in his *Journal* published in 1810, described descending the escarpment, but La Bajada didn't really enter infamy until much later—especially after it became the *only* direct route between Albuquerque and Santa Fe for automobiles.

A mile and a half of steep road, as tightly wound as an angry snake, paved with lava chunks with an attitude. A Tin Lizzie's nightmare.

One resident of La Bajada, the little village at the hill's base, recalled the time a driver, infuriated with his car's failure, pushed it over the cliff, then climbed down and shot it full of bullet holes.

Then there was the time a truckload of oranges upended on one of the many hairpin switchbacks. The site acquired the nickname Florida.

As motorists began trekking the continent in the 1920s, La Bajada became a landmark on the "Ocean to Ocean" highway. Drivers of Model Ts often backed up the hill to take advantage of a lower gear ratio and gravity feed for the fuel. La Bajada was where the radiator boiled over, where terrified children got out and walked, where oil pans were ruptured, where transmissions failed.

The late Henrietta Loy of Albuquerque was a young girl in the early 1920s. Her father was an optometrist—her grandfather had

LA BAJADA

The La Bajada road when it was in daily use. Courtesy of the Palace of the Governors Photo Archives, 008226.

been the state's first optometrist—and she accompanied him on deliveries. She remembered La Bajada well. "They had pullouts at the switchbacks where drivers could back up and get a run at the next section."

Once, her father took associates from Tennessee to Santa Fe. On the return trip, La Bajada eclipsed La Fonda on the Plaza, the landmark luxury hotel where they stayed in Santa Fe, in their memories of New Mexico. "Really, La Bajada was quite impressive."

La Bajada—complete with switchbacks, pullouts, and the skeletons of long-deceased vehicles—is still there, still impressive. And high-clearance four-wheel-drive vehicles can still muscle their way to the top, although they have to trespass on Cochiti Pueblo land to do so.

But these days La Bajada really belongs to hikers, especially those willing to linger over the route's details: the petroglyphs on the boulders, intriguing traces of indeterminate roads long abandoned, eagles and hawks riding the thermals sweeping up the cliffs, the 360-degree vistas spanning the valley of the Santa Fe River far below to the high peaks of the Sangre de Cristos.

Walkers get to experience this peace and quiet free from

CHAPTER SEVEN

The La Bajada road as it is today. Photo by Robert Julyan.

wondering if the scrapety-clunk from the vehicle's undercarriage means another automotive tragedy on La Bajada. This is perhaps the only hike in this book where no one is tempted to say, "I wish I was in a car."

Toponymic Note

Several people have pointed out to me that, to native Spanish speakers, the name La Bajada Hill isn't quite right, as it would mean "the downslope hill," but La Bajada Hill is the name in the US Geological Survey's Geographic Names Information System (GNIS) database, whose names are official for all federal publications, including maps. But as one who has long been involved in GNIS, I know that local usage often varies from the "official names," and in conversations I've never heard La Bajada Hill referred to as anything but La Bajada, so for most of this chapter that's the name I've used.

Getting There

Most people have done this hike from the bottom, from just southwest of the village of La Bajada (private property but with a public right-of-way running through it), parking on the east side of the river near the bridge, but because this route traverses land owned by Cochiti Pueblo, the only legal public access is from the top, over US Forest Service land. From Interstate 25 southwest of Santa Fe, take Relief Route 599 north to the second stoplight leading to Santa Fe Municipal Airport. Keep on the paved road, Paseo Real, 3.25 miles to unpaved County Road 56C. Follow this 0.75 miles until it crosses the public-land boundary. This road then ascends the mesa and runs for 7 miles from the boundary to the top of La Bajada, N 35 33 30 / W 106 13 31. But in September 2013, after weeks of unprecedented rain, I drove this route, and after 4.8 miles of dodging mudholes and bumpy, eroded dirt road I came to a gate saying that the road beyond was closed because of washout and "resource damage." I'm sure the road has since been restored, but check with the Forest Service first.

CHAPTER EIGHT

Mount Chalchihuitl

WHEN EUROPEANS ARRIVED in the Southwest, they discovered that the mineral the Native people valued above all others, beyond gold or silver, was the blue and green stone we know as turquoise. And for these early people the most important source of turquoise was a modest hill south of Santa Fe, appropriately named Chalchihuitl, the name used by the Nahuatl-speaking Aztecs for the stone. For more than a thousand years Indian peoples came here to quarry in tawny volcanic rock to collect fragments of the stone that not only was beautiful but also had powerful religious significance. They took the precious turquoise back to their settlements to fashion into ornaments and ritual objects, and they carried it over their trade networks. Centuries ago, a visitor would have heard the voices of Indian miners, the sound of stone hammers striking stone.

Today the hill is silent; Indian quarrying ceased long ago. Although chips and patches of turquoise, often looking like blue lichens, can still be found in the rubble around the mine, the turquoise used by modern Indians to make jewelry likely comes from China or one of several other nonlocal sources. In fact, although

CHAPTER EIGHT

New Mexico is closely associated with turquoise—the state stone—New Mexico has always been a minor player in turquoise production; it ranks last in modern turquoise production among the western states, and few if any of the state's seven turquoise mining operations are currently active. But when ancient Native Americans worked there, Mount Chalchihuitl was the Southwest's most extensive pre-European mining operation.

On a bright, hot day in early September I and my hiking partner, David Ryan, and his three adventure dogs, Teddy, Paddy, and Petey, set out to hike toward Mount Chalchihuitl. First we stopped in the village of Cerrillos and the visitors' center of Cerrillos Hills State Park, established in 2000, to get a map and an overview of the park. There, we're reminded that the park is much more than a gateway to Mount Chalchihuitl. It's a diverse and interesting natural area, and any person intending only to reach the hill will miss the best the park has to offer.

I also recommend going there to check on the access status. Until recently, Mount Chalchihuitl has been private property, but that is perhaps changing as I write this (see below).

Then we drove north over the normally dry bed of the Rio Galisteo, past the old Cerrillos Cemetery, to a picnic and parking area at the mouth of a narrow canyon. Two trailheads are here, slightly less than a mile apart, both connecting the Jane Calvin Sanchez Trail (this commemorates the noted New Mexico historian, 1929–2006, who was active in the Cerrillos Hills Park Coalition). We started at the lower one and would return to the upper one, at Cerrillos Spring.

One reason we chose the lower trailhead is that the analemma is here. Maintained by the park, it's a deceptively simple device not unlike a sundial that tracks the sun's movement during the year as it traces a graceful figure 8. I've read the interpretive panels half a dozen times and still don't understand the astronomical gyrations that cause the analemma phenomenon, but that's my fault. I'm sure it would have been child's play to the ancient astronomers of the Puebloan world.

MOUNT CHALCHIHUITL

Stereogram showing mining excavations at Mount Chalchihuitl in 1888. The cross on the summit was erected by D. C. Hyde. Photo by H. Milford, in the collection of Amigos de Cerrillos Hill State Park, courtesy of Homer Milford.

We approached Mount Chalchihuitl from the southwest, using hiking and horse trails maintained by Cerrillos Hills State Park. An arguably more authentic approach would have been from the east, from the direction of San Marcos Pueblo, now in ruins 2.5 miles from the hill. Archaeologists have found a five-room structure near Mount Chalchihuitl dating from AD 900 to AD 1100, which likely housed miners at the site. Those dates correlate approximately with the rise and fall of Chacoan civilization, at whose sites turquoise from Mount Chalchihuitl has been found. But with the collapse of Chaco and its satellites around AD 1250, mining at Mount Chalchihuitl became dominated by the Rio Grande pueblos, notably San Marcos.

As we started up the trail, a wide track based on one of the park's many old roads, we noticed a smaller track worn in the center, with horseshoe imprints and horse droppings; horseback riding is the park's main recreational use.

The hiking was straightforward and relatively easy, but as we

CHAPTER EIGHT

hiked I was reminded that history can be hard on the land, especially when mining is involved. The ground has been chewed up by roads and excavations; prospect pits and old mines are everywhere; and the ground is littered with angular fragments of volcanic andesite-latite porphyry—mining debris. In appearance, this rock reminds me of rocky road ice cream, dark flecks in a creamy mass.

This, along with latite and monzonite, are the igneous rocks that intruded into much older sedimentary rocks beginning about thirty-four million years ago. The uplift fractured the rocks involved, and about twenty-nine million years ago mineral-rich solutions filled the cracks, producing the veins of metal ore that attracted miners. The turquoise, however, came much later. No earlier than three to four million years ago, chemical changes near the subsurface water table created turquoise deposits.

While much of the weathered and rusted debris from abandoned American mining now resides in the Turquoise Mining Museum in Cerrillos, you can still see broken glass and rusted metal beneath the widely scattered piñon and juniper trees.

Mining devours a lot of wood, and throughout the park are the weathered gray stumps of trees cut more than a hundred years ago. Some stumps and branches have clean, sawn ends; others with ragged ends were cut earlier by axes. Almost all of this dates from American mining in the Cerrillos Hills in the late nineteenth century.

Although the ancient Indians did mine here to extract galena, a lead ore used to glaze their pottery, their primary interest was in turquoise, from Mount Chalchihuitl and other mines.

When the Spaniards arrived around 1600, they scoffed at the Indians for their fixation on the blue and green stone—just as Indians scoffed at the Spaniards' obsession with a certain soft yellow metal—but while the conquistadores didn't find in the Cerrillos Hills the gold they most desired, they did find silver as well as other metals, notably lead.

Apocryphal stories persist that the Spaniards used Indian slaves to extract turquoise at Mount Chalchihuitl, but no solid evidence corroborates this. Perhaps the strongest, albeit indirect, evidence that post-Spanish Indians worked the turquoise mines at Mount Chalchihuitl is the name itself: the Nahuatl-speaking Tlaxcalan Indians the Spaniards brought from Mexico as laborers would have referred to the hill as Chalchihuitl when mining turquoise there.

Similarly, it's likely a fiction that turquoise from Mount Chalchihuitl was traded to the Aztecs in central Mexico. As Joe Dan Lowry of the Turquoise Museum in Albuquerque's Old Town asks, why would the Aztecs import turquoise from New Mexico when abundant local sources were available?

In fact, Mount Chalchihuitl was largely forgotten until the arrival in 1857 of the geologist William P. Blake. He met Navajos possessing turquoise, but they obtained it from Pueblo Indians, who directed him to Mount Chalchihuitl. He was hugely impressed by the diggings and publicized them with effusive nineteenth-century hyperbole. It was through his writings that Mount Chalchihuitl became famous and the subject of myths, arguably to its detriment.

Most evidence of Spanish mining in the Cerrillos Hills, including Mount Chalchihuitl, was obliterated when American mining began in earnest in 1879; Robert Hart reopened old Spanish silver workings and recruited miners from Leadville, Colorado. And as was typical of such discoveries throughout the American West in the late 1800s, a mining boom ensued. Prospectors swarmed the Cerrillos Hills like ants on a picnic cake. Mining camps sprang up with names like Carbonateville, Purdins Camp, and Poverty Hollow; and, when the railroad arrived in 1880, the village of Cerrillos (originally Los Cerrillos) was born. (This is not to be confused with the Los Cerrillos founded in the late seventeenth century by don Diego de Vargas northwest of the Cerrillos hills.)

Within half a mile of hiking, David and I had encountered the first of many abandoned mines, fenced and capped for safety. But everywhere were smaller holes and pits that didn't make it to mine status, each spewing rocky debris.

The land here has been used—hard.

CHAPTER EIGHT

We came here in September, and by midmorning the temperature was already climbing. The three dogs kept gravitating toward any hint of shade. The arroyos were all dry. Where, I wondered, did the miners obtain water?

And what of the plants and animals that live here? We hiked during a period of drought. The vegetation was sere, withered. The only green was on the evergreen species—piñon pines, oneseed junipers, Gambel oak, scrub oak. But in a wetter season the land would have been verdant and colorful with trees such as chokecherry, coyote willow, New Mexico locust, and wavyleaf oak, with wildflowers such as sunflower, blanketflower, blue trumpet, purslane, Easter daisy, globe mallow, purple locoweed, paintbrush, Perky Sue, and many others.

The trails are exposed to wind and sun. Animals are here, but many are nocturnal or hiding in the shade: striped skunk, bobcats, gray fox, kangaroo rats, and numerous small rodents. In sandy arroyos are tracks of deer and coyotes. Black bears live here. So do horned lizards, collared lizards, frogs and toads, and five species of snakes, including western diamondback and prairie rattlesnakes. These too are mostly nocturnal.

Conspicuously nocturnal are bats. Four species of bats use the abandoned mines as their homes, and simply filling or capping the mines to protect humans would destroy the bat colonies. That's why mines identified as having bats are covered with grates or netting.

Eventually we reached Mount Chalchihuitl. Topographically indistinguishable from the area's other "little hills"—littler, in fact, than most—I recognize it by the pit carved crudely into its north side and the numerous old roads and tracks converging on it. In the rock rubble surrounding the hill I find flecks of turquoise. To preserve these from souvenir hunters—and to protect visitors who might clamber over the unstable rock faces and holes—the park restricts access to the hill itself.

Poor Mount Chalchihuitl. It has suffered grievously from its fame. Not only has it been mutilated physically, but also its reputation was sullied when in 1880 D. C. Hyde acquired the property and began selling stock to eastern investors. They would receive the profits of gold and silver mining at the legendary ancient mine—despite no gold or silver ever having been found there. Another western mining scam. At the time, turquoise was worthless, except to mineral collectors and Native Americans.

That changed, however, in the late 1880s when European interest in turquoise revived as Persian sources were exhausted. Prices rose precipitously until at one time turquoise was worth more per ounce than gold. Mines were developed not only in the Cerrillos Hills—the Tiffany Mine was operated by the famous New York jewelers—but throughout the West, and most were far more productive than Mount Chalchihuitl.

But the boom was ephemeral. Within a decade prices were falling, and by 1912 the market had collapsed. Turquoise is still valuable, especially to Indian jewelers, but it's more economical for them to buy turquoise imported from China and elsewhere.

So today Mount Chalchihuitl, like nearby San Marcos Pueblo, is inhabited only by ghosts and valuable only for the history it represents.

We hiked back over a landscape that shows the wear and tear it has endured. But human history, like climate, is ever changing. With protection by the state park the land will recover, and with rains the vegetation will turn green again.

The Jane Calvin Sanchez Trail took us to Cerrillos Spring. Once reduced to just a seep by human activity and overgrazing, the spring's restoration was among the park's first projects, and when we arrived water was flowing, riparian plants were green, and dragonflies darted around. The Cerrillos Hills and Mount Chalchihuitl are entering a new phase of their history.

San Marcos Pueblo

From its beginning around AD 1300 to its abandonment after the Pueblo Revolt of 1680, San Marcos, the largest of the Rio Grande pueblos with approximately two thousand ground-floor rooms,

CHAPTER EIGHT

dominated turquoise mining at Mount Chalchihuitl. Archaeologists studying turquoise pits south of Mount Chalchihuitl found that 75 percent of the potsherds found there came from San Marcos—and 95 percent of them date from 1300 to 1600. But without doubt other pueblos also visited the site; historic records show inhabitants of Santo Domingo, Cochiti, San Felipe, and San Ildefonso all working the mines.

These Indians exploited area turquoise deposits other than Mount Chalchihuitl, but subsequent disturbance, especially by nineteenth-century American prospectors, has made it difficult to estimate their extent.

Today, San Marcos sleeps just north of San Marcos Arroyo and immediately east of NM 14. It is protected as an archaeological site with limited public access.

A little about sourcing turquoise: Turquoise is conspicuously variable. It should be simple to look at a piece of turquoise at an archaeological site and use appearance and geochemistry to determine its source, but it doesn't work that way. To emphasize the point, Joe Dan Lowry of the Turquoise Museum in Albuquerque took me to a display case with several beautiful turquoise specimens—sky blue, pale green, blue green, other shades. "They all came from the same source, just a few feet from each other," he said.

Frances Joan Mathien, adjunct professor of anthropology at the University of New Mexico, and her colleagues have been chipping away at the problem of using chemical analysis to source turquoise. It's more complex than it might seem, but they're making progress. They've learned that while turquoise at places like Chaco Canyon may have come from the Cerrillos Hills, it didn't necessarily come from Mount Chalchihuitl itself. Some turquoise at Chaco came from the Castillian Mine, at the range's north end. There are numerous turquoise deposits in the Cerrillos Hills, including the Tiffany Mine, now closed, on Turquoise Hill to the north.

This has led Mathien to ask deeper questions about the Puebloan turquoise trade:

Who in Chaco obtained the turquoise, through what networks? Were all the people in Chaco working in the same set of networks, or were there several groups linked to different trade networks? Because potsherds at Cerrillos (several mines including those in the northern section at Castillian) reflect different groups, how do we know who went to mine, who traded with perhaps relatives or lineage members living in other communities, etc.? Guess I am a bit more skeptical of a straight line between Chaco and Cerrillos.

As for the site's ownership status, until recently Mount Chalchihuitl was privately owned, with no public access, but in 2013 Santa Fe County voters approved a bond issue that would allow for incorporation of the hill into Cerrillos Hills State Park. That's great news, but public access to the hill will remain restricted to prevent scavenging by souvenir hunters and for the safety of visitors; rocks making up the old workings are very unstable. Also, several other private inholdings in the park block access to the hill itself. Be sure to check the visitors' center in Cerrillos for the latest information.

Persons wanting samples of Mount Chalchihuitl turquoise should visit shops in Cerrillos and Madrid or the Turquoise Museum in Albuquerque. They have better samples than you can find on your own.

Toponymic Note

As someone interested in place names, it has not escaped my notice that the name "Cerrillos Hills" is redundant, as the Spanish *cerrillos* means "little hills." Something like the Rio Grande River, Picacho Peak, and Table Mesa.

To Learn More

Visit the Cerrillos Hills State Park Visitors' Center in Cerrillos, (505) 474-0196, or visit the park's extremely informative website,

CHAPTER EIGHT

www.cerrilloshills.org. There is a very active schedule of outings and events related to the park.

Visit the Cerrillos Turquoise Mining Museum, 17 Waldo Street, Cerrillos, (505) 438-3008, established and operated by Todd and Patricia Brown; there's lots of fascinating local history. They can answer just about any questions you might have.

Visit the Turquoise Museum in Albuquerque, 2707 Central Avenue NW, (505) 247-8650. Take one of their tours, and visit their website. Also, read Joe Dan Lowry and Joe P. Lowry's *Turquoise: The World Story of a Fascinating Gemstone* (Layton, UT: Gibbs Smith, 2010), or *Turquoise Unearthed: An Illustrated Guide* (Tucson, AZ: Rio Nuevo Publishers, 2002) by the same authors. Joe P. Lowry founded the Turquoise Museum and writes in collaboration with his son, Joe Dan. You don't know turquoise unless you've been there.

Read William Baxter's book, *The Gold of the Ortiz Mountains: A Story of New Mexico and the West's First Major Gold Rush* (Santa Fe, NM: Lone Butte Press, 2004). Mount Chalchihuitl and San Marcos Pueblo are almost one story, and no one knew it better than William Baxter.

CHAPTER NINE

The Story of Sam the Dinosaur

THIS IS A story of a dinosaur named Sam. The name was chosen because it could refer either to a male (Samuel) or a female (Samantha), handy because we don't know Sam's gender. In fact, that we know anything at all about Sam, including that the dinosaur existed at all, is a testament to the power of serendipity.

The story begins in 1979 with two Albuquerque hikers, Arthur Loy and Jan Cummings. Arthur was a well-known music educator and promoter of music in New Mexico; Jan, a pharmacist, had been trained as a geologist. But both really were "wanderers" in the highest sense of the word: people always putting themselves in the way of discovering the world's unexpected wonders.

On the day of Sam's discovery in what is now the Ojito Wilderness, they were not wandering randomly but rather hiking and photographing with a purpose. The Bureau of Land Management and even some wilderness advocates had dropped the Ojito area northwest of Albuquerque from consideration for wilderness status; Jan and Arthur and others disagreed with the decision. On an earlier solo hike in the Ojito, Jan had noticed petroglyphs atop a

CHAPTER NINE

bluff. Knowing that archaeological sites would tip the scales toward wilderness designation, the two returned to the site to photograph the rock art. As Jan tells the story:

> It was while paralleling me (our usual way of exploring) about fifty feet below the mesa edge that he [Arthur] called to me—"Jan, come see what you make of this." While walking toward Arthur I instantly recognized from thirty feet the obvious vertebrae of a large dinosaur. The articulated vertebral column looked like a huge chicken neck laying half in and half out of sandstone. Right off it seemed likely that they were from a sauropod about the size of *Diplodocus*. It was my impression that there were lots of these giants in Utah, Colorado, and Wyoming, so I didn't think it unique, although I knew from all my years hiking in New Mexico that this was a rare find. (Arthur told me that he had never found even a piece of dinosaur bone before.)

(I, too, have spent many years hiking in New Mexico, in the same places Jan and Arthur hiked. I have even hiked with them. I have never found a dinosaur bone here.)

"Now what to do about the discovery?" Jan remembered kidding Arthur. "I'm sure glad it's your responsibility, since you found it."

Jan and Arthur took their hiking partner Frank Walker to the site. Then they went to the Bureau of Land Management (BLM), which administered the land. Their paleontologist, Keith Rigby, was excited and instantly recognized the find's importance. But then he left to take a new position out of state.

The dinosaur was forgotten except by the discoverers and their friends. Bill Norlander, a television news expert, videotaped the site. By 1985 dirt bikers and woodcutters were discovering the Ojito area. Jan and Arthur were worried. They contacted Jon Callendar, director of the New Mexico Museum of Natural History and Science, and arrangements were made for Dennis Umshler, the BLM's

THE STORY OF SAM THE DINOSAUR

Sam the *Seismosaurus* in the New Mexico Museum of Natural History and Science. Photo by David Ryan.

paleontology coordinator, and David D. Gillette, the museum's paleontologist, to visit the site.

"I was transfixed by the bones," Gillette later wrote, "not because of their size—that realization would come later—but because of how remarkably well preserved they were and because they were still connected."

A week later, the local TV evening news carried the story. Jan says, "When we reexamined the site we found it covered with human footprints of all sizes. Excavation was put on fast track by the BLM and museum."

Over the next several years, Gillette organized scientists and volunteers to excavate the bones and look for others. Scientists from the Los Alamos National Laboratory provided ground-penetrating radar and other new technologies to search within the dense sandstone. Ultimately, several other bones belonging to Sam were

CHAPTER NINE

recovered, though not the entire skeleton; among the missing bones were the legs and the head.

The fossil needed a name for workers to use; Gillette suggested Sam. And Sam also needed a scientific name; Gillette chose *Seismosaurus hallii*, later *Seismosaurus hallorum*, the species name honoring the Reverend James Hall, director of the Ghost Ranch Conference Center, and his wife, Ruth, both pioneering amateur paleontologists in New Mexico.

As for *Seismosaurus*, "Earth Shaker," Gillette chose it because, based on preliminary estimates, the creature could very well have been the world's largest dinosaur—and certainly New Mexico's—larger even than the recently discovered Ultrasaurus and Supersaurus. (One wag suggested the name *Sooperdoopersaurus*.)

Seismosaurus was indeed, after further study, proclaimed the world's largest dinosaur and became an instant celebrity. She or he was the superstar at a 2002 exhibit of the bones of the world's largest dinosaurs. Since then, larger dinosaurs have been discovered, and new measurements of Sam have reduced Sam's size somewhat and even taken away the genus name, *Seismosaurus*, arguing that the creature isn't entirely sui generis but rather an individual of the genus *Diplodocus*. That Sam was a diplodocus seems clear, but beyond that, the arguments are complex and technical. For most New Mexicans, however, Sam will always be *Seismosaurus*, just as Pluto will always be a planet.

And Sam remains a remarkable discovery, as articulated dinosaur remains are extremely rare. The paleontologists discovered more than 240 rounded, sometimes waxy stones, from one to four inches in diameter, at two places in Sam's skeleton. These gastroliths were kept in the dinosaur's digestive tract to help grind tough plant material, much as birds keep grit in their crops to grind seeds. That they were found inside the skeleton meant that they were revealed as the carcass decayed—and that meant the articulated bones and gastroliths stayed together after Sam's death. Very likely Sam's bones were found close to the place of death, rather than being dispersed by a stream in flooding or by waves on a beach.

THE STORY OF SAM THE DINOSAUR

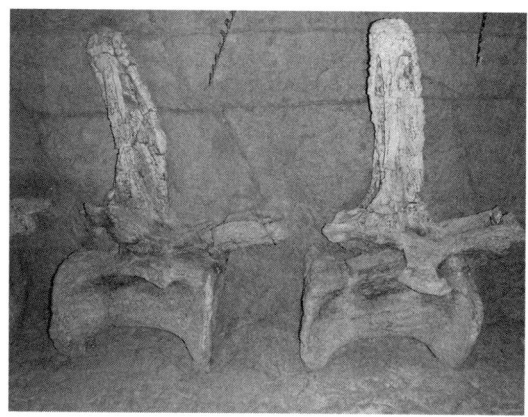

The fossilized vertebrae discovered by Jan Cummings and Arthur Loy. Photo by Robert Julyan.

(To see Sam's bones today, visit the New Mexico Museum of Natural History and Science.)

Sam lived a very long time ago, during the late Jurassic Period, long before Cabezon (a nearby volcano) erupted, before the ridges folded, even before North America existed as a continent, when to the north was a large sea and the barren, dry region that today forms New Mexico lay just north of the equator. Numerous north-flowing rivers and streams drained land vegetated by conifers and ferns and cycads; flowering plants had not yet appeared. A time almost unimaginably long ago. When the footfalls of giant sauropod dinosaurs shook the earth.

How did Sam die? We can't know, but a single carnivorous dinosaur tooth was discovered near Sam's remains. Did the carnivore attack Sam? Or scavenge the carcass? Or was the tooth washed in before or after Sam was mere bones? We can't know, unless new evidence is found, such as tooth marks on newly discovered bone.

But the story of Sam is more than just bones; it's also the story of their discovery, a story we can relive by visiting where the discovery took place, because what happened to Arthur and Jan could happen to any of us, especially in a place like the Ojito Wilderness.

I first encountered the *Seismosaurus* site on the second day of a

CHAPTER NINE

two-day backpacking trip into the wilderness from the west with the outdoor photographer William Stone. We'd spent the night atop Bernalillito Mesa. Hiking there, we found the decaying remains of hundred-year-old homesteader cabins, along with their sad and broken windmills.

Atop the mesa and elsewhere in the wilderness were small clusters of stone-and-adobe room blocks and field houses, built perhaps a thousand years ago by Indians. Along with mounds of rubble, they left behind sherds of pottery used to store grain, manos and metates to grind it, flakes of nonlocal flint, and petroglyphs pecked onto flat sandstone surfaces. Like the homesteaders, they'd fought a hard battle to wrest a living from a harsh land, failed, and moved on.

The next day we hiked across the valley. Because Bill is a photographer, we stopped often, something I regard as a perquisite of hiking with photographers. They force me to stop and really be present where I am, instead of just moving through the land as I often do. We both remarked that rarely had we been in a place with such a high density of interest. Odd geological formations. Very deep arroyos. Sheets of calcite crystals. Petrified wood. Archaeological artifacts. Desert plants in bloom.

We climbed a sandstone mesa across the valley. On a prominent bluff we found more petroglyphs—and where Sam's bones had once resided. We'd seen no people, no signs, no roads, and no trails. Arthur and Jan were right: this was indeed wilderness and has been formally so designated by Congress. Bill had known the location of this site and had been guiding us.

Today, getting to the *Seismosaurus* site is much easier than a two-day backpack.

From Interstate 25, take US 550 west and northwest from Bernalillo 21.75 miles, about 2 miles before the village of San Ysidro. Just beneath the conspicuous white mesa on your left, a dirt road branches left (west) and forks almost immediately; continue straight ahead, through lands belonging to the Zia Indian Reservation (no trespassing). After 4.1 miles, you come to a sign saying you're entering public land. After about 10 miles from US 550 is an informal parking area on your left (N 35 29 44.5 / W 106 54 24) and across the road a pass-through to a trail heading north one mile toward the *Seismosaurus* site (N 35 30 21 / W 106 54 39). Appropriately, neither the parking area nor the trail are marked. After all, this is wilderness.

The Ojito Wilderness is a land that's arid and desiccated. It's named for a "little spring" on Zia Indian Reservation land, which is off-limits; I know of no other springs in the vicinity. This land looks old, weathered. The plants here are of the Upper Sonoran life zone—saltbush, mountain mahogany, juniper, snakeweed, cane cholla cactus—barely able to subsist on not very much. Like the people who once lived here.

But it's the landforms that command attention. The tawny sandstone sculpted into fantastic shapes, often called hoodoos, by grains of sand driven by wind and by infrequent drops of rain falling from time out of mind. Multicolored bare hills reminiscent of the Painted Desert. In the distance looms the giant black stump of Cabezon, the largest of several volcanic plugs resulting from when the Mount Taylor volcanic field erupted along the Rio Puerco valley about 2.5 million years ago. Lava surged upward through vents in the overlying rocks, which, when later eroded, left standing giant plugs of black volcanic basalt. Along the trail are pieces of basalt ejected from the eruptions, or carried here by people much later. Usually they are porous, like black sponges, evidence of gas bubbles once inside.

All around are mesas and bluffs, most capped by light-colored sandstone underlaid by softer reddish-brownish siltstone deposits—regular, predictable, orderly. This is the Morrison Formation. When Sam's enormous feet shook the earth here, the sand was a beach, likely along a stream flowing north toward an ancient sea. Nearby grew giant ferns and cycads; flowering plants did not exist then. Extensive mud flats then became siltstone. During the Jurassic Period, North America did not exist as a continent; the land was close to the equator, and none of the features we see today existed. Such is the depth of geologic time.

CHAPTER NINE

It soon becomes obvious that the trail follows what once was a two-track road, used by excavators before wilderness designation. The rock underfoot is typically very hard sandstone. As you approach the bluff, you notice strange linear rock formations that resemble giant petrified logs. They aren't. I don't have a clue how they formed. Other strange shapes appear.

And then you're at the site, a sandstone bluff encircled by cliffs, with a sand-filled concavity gouged in its south side near the top. Here is where Sam was discovered, where the bones were excavated. Around the site are angular blocks, remnants of the excavation.

Look around, then climb to the desert-varnished horizontal rocks atop the bluff, to the surfaces on which ancient Indians pecked enigmatic petroglyphs.

And don't stop even here, for if ever a place was welcoming to wanderers, it's the Ojito Wilderness. Having no trails to follow compels wandering; having no particular destination encourages slowing down. So follow your curiosity off-trail into the wilderness, as Arthur and Jan so often did.

Could you also discover dinosaur bones? Sure. The Morrison Formation outcrops in several places throughout the wilderness, and not all of them have been examined. Besides, nature shuffles the cards and redeals the hands with each rainstorm. What was hidden a week ago is visible now. You could even discover more of Sam's bones. Still, I wouldn't plan your trip around finding dinosaur bones.

But I can guarantee that you'll find something interesting: Indian artifacts or calcite crystals or petrified wood or ancient seashells or weird marble-like concretions or a thousand other unexpected wonders. And remember: dinosaurs aren't the only fossils here. Shells and fossilized wood are abundant. By getting out, opening your eyes and your mind, you'll never be disappointed.

As a reminder: because the ecosystem here is very fragile, especially on exposed soil, tread lightly—and take only photographs.

THE STORY OF SAM THE DINOSAUR

Yes, It Can Happen

I know one other person who came across dinosaur bones while hiking in the backcountry. David Love, senior geologist with the New Mexico Bureau of Geology in Socorro, was hiking up an arroyo, certainly not looking for fossils but not unaware of them either, when he suddenly saw bones in the arroyo's eroded wall. While not a paleontologist, he nonetheless recognized them as belonging to a dinosaur. No, the discovery didn't create the stir that Sam's did, but they were dinosaur bones nonetheless.

Actually, when I was a college freshman, *I* found dinosaur bones. East of Boulder, Colorado, a reservoir where I fished had released a lot of water, exposing the shoreline. There were the bones of a long dinosaur, and since I'd always been obsessed with dinosaurs and knew something about them, I suspected a mosasaur. I took a fragment to a paleontologist at the University of Colorado Department of Geology. He glanced at the bone, said, "Looks like a mosasaur," and returned to shuffling papers. He had no interest in how I'd come by the bone, although I was eager to tell him.

A disgrace to science!

Postscript

Years of patient, persistent work by the New Mexico Wilderness Alliance paid off in 2005 when Congress created the 11,183-acre Ojito Wilderness.

A Worthwhile Side Trip

About thirty-five million years ago, continent-scale movements pushed and twisted deep sedimentary layers like a rumpled bedsheet. This created the anticlines—recognized here by ridges looking like a sliced watermelon. The Tierra Amarilla anticline is the most dramatic, and geologists come from all over to see it. It is four miles from US 550 on the dirt road leading to the *Seismosaurus* site; look for a parking area on your right, then head uphill to an overlook. It's well worth the trip.

Personal Note

I have been privileged to know Jan Cummings and Arthur Loy personally and have hiked with both of them. No, I didn't go with them to the Ojito, and no, we didn't find more dinosaur bones, but we *always* found *something*. That's the real lesson of the Ojito Wilderness. And for more of the philosophy that led to Jan and Arthur's discovery, I highly recommend a book by my archaeology and wandering partner, David Ryan, called *The Gentle Art of Wandering* (Albuquerque, NM: New Mountain Books, 2012).

To Learn More

Visit the New Mexico Museum of Natural History and Science, 1801 Mountain Road NW, Albuquerque, New Mexico, (505) 841-2800. Here you'll find Sam's bones as Arthur and Jan found them, as well as a very impressive reconstruction of Sam's complete skeleton. A must for dinosaur lovers.

Read *Seismosaurus: The Earth Shaker*, by David D. Gillette (New York: Columbia University Press, 1994). Gillette was in charge of the excavation of Sam's fossil. The book includes stunning illustrations by Mark Hallett and numerous photographs.

CHAPTER TEN

Bomb Targets on New Mexico's Mesas

TIME IS ERASING New Mexico's World War II bomb targets, just as the bomb craters in Europe are filling in, just as people's memories of the war are fading, just as the people who lived through the war are dying. On New Mexico's mesa tops and plains, the bull's-eyes and cross hairs now are barely visible on aerial photographs, and on the ground they vanish completely among the cholla, saltbush, and rabbitbrush, while the bomb fragments themselves, once painted bright blue, are now rusting to dark brown. Prairie dogs seem to have an affinity for the targets, constructing their mounds and burrows among the bomb fragments and other debris. With each human generation, the bomb targets will be harder and harder to find.

I had no idea that World War II bomb targets existed in New Mexico until my archaeology partner and I were using Google Earth to survey a remote area southwest of Albuquerque. On top of a sprawling mesa were three barely visible concentric circles, separated by many miles, the largest about fifty yards in diameter.

CHAPTER TEN

On our next trip we looked for one—and could not find it on the ground. We later returned with GPS way points obtained from Google Earth and were able to find the low, eroded, scrub-covered berms making up the target. Going to the center, we found increasing numbers of bomb fragments. Most were barely recognizable, but soon we could discern the detonation assemblies and tail fins, each about the size of a small mailbox.

Later I learned that World War II bomb targets exist throughout New Mexico, used from 1942 to 1945 by training missions out of Albuquerque, Hobbs, Carlsbad, Roswell, and Deming. I have been to four bomb targets, all likely used by pilots from Kirtland Air Force Base. Most were remote and relatively difficult to reach.

And none more so than a bomb target we discovered by accident in the Ojito Wilderness northwest of Albuquerque. At the base of a large mesa we came upon the telltale metal fragments. Later, my friend used Google Earth to get coordinates for the bull's-eye, then scrambled to the mesa's top and located the target. I needed to see it for myself, so he gave me the coordinates, and one bright winter's day I set out.

I drove on US 550 until about 2.4 miles from the village of San Ysidro. I turned west on a dirt road at a sign indicating the Ojito Wilderness, driving through land belonging to the Zia Indian Reservation until, at 4.1 miles from US 550, I entered public land administered by the Bureau of Land Management. As described in chapter 9, the geology is dramatic: water-chiseled ridges and wind-sculpted outcrops of multicolored sandstone—tan, brown, yellow, red. Beneath the cliffs are slopes of pink, maroon, and dark-brown siltstone and mudstone, remnants of ancient tidal flats, beaches, and streams. But the water that shaped this landscape has receded into the almost unimaginable remoteness of geologic time; the only water here now is a single manmade pond for cattle.

At 4.6 miles is the parking area for the Tierra Amarilla anticline, a deep, narrow valley in whose bottom mineral-laden springs have

Concrete-filled practice bombs on Albuquerque's West Mesa. Photo by Robert Julyan.

created travertine domes, a favorite destination for hikers, mountain bikers, and geologists on field trips.

Then, at 8.5 miles (N 35 28 58.2 / W 106 53 24.5), just as the road begins to dip into a shallow valley just past the pond, I parked where a smaller dirt road heads west. Time to begin hiking.

I walked on the smaller dirt road as it bent south around a small wetland to arrive soon at a fence that runs arrow-straight toward a large mesa to the west. The fence stops at cliffs, but I saw a small cairn on the mesa's top and then what appears to be a cleft in the cliffs. It's a scramble to get up it, but at the top I was rewarded with spectacular views of the red cliffs leading to Jemez Pueblo, of the escarpment of the Sierra Nacimiento, and everywhere to the north and west the vast and beautiful Ojito Wilderness.

Almost immediately on the mesa top I found bomb fragments, chunks of rusted metal no larger than a cigar box, jagged and

CHAPTER TEN

twisted upon impact. My GPS unit indicated that the target was still half a mile away—could some bombardiers have been that inaccurate?

No landmarks exist on the mesa top, no trails, no rock outcrops; even the junipers are widely scattered. On satellite images, the bull's-eye is so faint that it's not apparent even when you're looking right at it. On the ground, it's totally invisible. Without GPS coordinates (N 35 29 03.2 / W 106 54 42.4) to guide me to it, I had no hope of finding the target. I meandered through scrub—saltbush, snakeweed, cholla, prickly pear cactus, and yucca. The increasing density of bomb fragments told me I was getting closer.

And then there it was. A low mound, twenty feet in diameter, five feet high; without the rusted iron scattered over it, it would just look like a prairie dog abode, which in fact it was. A few gray, weathered boards were nearby, as were fragments of glass, their origin unknown. As I hiked to the mesa's edge to return by a different route, I continued finding bomb fragments, even at the mesa's base. What bombardier couldn't even hit a mesa that was bigger than most airports?

But don't get the impression that if you've seen one bomb target, you've seen them all. Most are bull's-eyes, 1,000 to 1,800 feet in diameter, created by using a bulldozer blade to scrape away the earth, but others were demarcated using stones. And a few also have gunsight cross hairs in the center, the cross hairs occasionally twisted into swastikas or reverse swastikas. Other bomb targets represent ships, ship docks, and oil-storage tanks. Arguably the most elaborate targets were associated with Roswell Army Air Field. Over half of the thirty-four RAAF targets are either swastikas or reverse swastikas superimposed over a bull's-eye target. Large berms six feet high, fifteen feet wide, and a thousand feet long form the cross hairs in the center of the target. Small appendages placed halfway down and perpendicular to each leg complete the appearance of the swastika.

Take that, Nazis!

BOMB TARGETS ON NEW MEXICO'S MESAS

Based upon a visual reconstruction of the fragments, most of bombs were ten-pounders of a type known as BDU 48/B. The firing pin assembly was the bomb part that most often survived impact, although sometimes the canister and the tail fins can be identified. At the Ojito bomb target are the nose pieces of larger, heavier bombs.

The bombs were designed so that impact drove a firing pin into a shotgun shell mounted in the tail assembly, which then fired into a charge of black powder, releasing a puff of black smoke allowing air crews to evaluate the drop's accuracy. The detonation could not have been very powerful—I've never seen even the smallest impact crater—but then these were practice bombs. Some training missions dropped hundred-pound bombs filled with concrete or sand; a small spotting charge detonated upon impact, flashing flame and smoke. Sometimes other weaponry such as high-explosive, water-filled chemical bombs and incendiary bombs were used. I've never seen evidence of those.

I hiked off the mesa to return to my car. The air was calm; Albuquerque was but a distant smear on the horizon, and I was beyond the reach of highway noise from US 550. Even more remote were images of a war in Europe, the drone of bombers approaching their targets, the bombs falling, the explosions, fire and smoke. I was reminded as I hiked through the wilderness that in the sound and fury of human affairs, time and silence ultimately win.

An Easily Accessible Bomb Target

If you'd like to see a bomb target without climbing a mesa in the wilderness—although that experience is very worthwhile—you can go to the Petroglyph National Monument on Albuquerque's West Mesa. It's a short, easy hike to the site, whose coordinates are N 36 08 23 / W 106 46 03.5. This site is notable in that the old bombs here are larger and more complete than at other sites.

CHAPTER TEN

Respect the Site

Don't remove any bomb fragments or other debris from any bomb target. Because they are more than fifty years old, they are classified as cultural artifacts, and their disturbance or removal is illegal.

CHAPTER ELEVEN

The Crash of TWA Flight 260

SNOW HAD BEEN falling on the morning of February 19, 1955, and the ten-thousand-foot crest of the Sandia Mountains was obscured by clouds. At the Albuquerque airport, a TWA Martin 404 airliner, seventy-five feet long with a ninety-three-foot wingspan, taxied out to the runway to begin its trans-American journey to Baltimore, Maryland. The airplane, Skyliner Binghamton N-4016, had arrived the evening before. This morning's flight would terminate at 10:40 p.m. in Baltimore, with numerous intermediate stops en route. The first would be in Santa Fe, a twenty-six-minute hop from Albuquerque.

There was light snow and low clouds, but nothing to concern Ivan Spong, captain of Flight 260. He had twelve years of experience with TWA, including more than a hundred transatlantic flights during World War II. He'd logged almost 13,000 hours as a pilot, at least 1,500 of them flying in the clouds by instruments. He'd flown this particular route many times, in all weather. In fact, this trip between the two New Mexico cities would be his twelfth this month.

CHAPTER ELEVEN

At precisely 7:05 a.m., Spong shoved the throttle forward. The plane lifted off. Eight minutes later, he and the other fifteen persons on board would be dead.

The crash of TWA Flight 260 on a ridge high on the western face of the Sandia Mountains remains New Mexico's greatest air disaster. Even today, more than half a century later, visiting the site evokes a powerful sense of tragedy. Wreckage still litters the ground in a confined, rocky canyon, a cold place whose jagged granite ridges block the sun.

The hike into TWA Canyon is among the most scenic in the Sandias—and the one I am most reluctant to take.

I begin the hike from the Elena Gallegos Picnic Area, about two miles east of Tramway Boulevard. I've paid the modest parking fee, which allows backpackers to leave their vehicles in safety should they wish to spend the night in the wilderness. I've done this hike several times, so I don't really need the signs indicating the Domingo Baca Trail. Besides, I recognize Domingo Baca Canyon to the northeast by the gray, granite cliffs hedging the deep, narrow canyon. If that weren't enough, I'd recognize the canyon by the Sandia tramcars shuttling on their cables high overhead.

The trail starts in Albuquerque Open Space, crosses the sandy arroyo issuing from Pino Canyon directly east, then follows a network of dirt roads and mountain-biking trails before entering the US Forest Service's Sandia Mountain Wilderness. The area is very popular with hikers, trail runners, and mountain bikers, so it's easy to lose the main trail, but the canyon's mouth (approximately N 35 10 43 / W 106 27 46) remains an obvious objective. I know I've arrived when I see, just before the mouth, the ruins of a small stone cabin. A shelter for a Hispanic sheepherder—perhaps named Domingo Baca? Or perhaps his name was Juan Tabo? His identity remains a mystery.

Confined by near-vertical canyon walls, a tiny stream flows. In a normal year its waters sink into the arroyo's sand within half a mile of the canyon's mouth, but in the canyon itself the stream is one

Debris remaining in TWA Canyon from the plane crash. Photo by Gerry Sussman.

of the most reliable on the mountains' west side. The vegetation it waters is lush: horsetail rushes, mint, cottonwoods, and, lurking near the trail junction ahead, poison ivy. For about a quarter of a mile a skein of narrow routes parallels the stream, then at a junction frequently missed (N 35 10 43 / W 106 27 13) the route abruptly jogs right and climbs a short, steep, eroding bank. At the top, the trail becomes obvious again.

Here in a dry, open flat I pause and look upward. The cliffs above are stark, rugged. Climbers have named them all. The image that comes to mind is of teeth; the pinnacle that the airplane struck is named Dragon Tooth.

The trail leaves the meadow to enter another constricted canyon, again with a tiny stream. Huge, gnarly oaks surround an obvious campsite. I and my two daughters know it well; in fact, I often refer to it as the best place in the Sandias to introduce children to backpacking.

The trail parallels the stream for a quarter mile to arrive at a T-junction (N 35 11 06 / W 106 27 30). The right branch heads

CHAPTER ELEVEN

upward into what has become known as TWA Canyon. Until this point, the hiking has been relatively easy, but now the trail becomes steeper. Gone are the piñons and junipers of the foothills; the bear grass and mountain mahogany and prickly pear and cholla cacti are replaced by ponderosa pines and, still higher, Douglas fir and white spruce. Distant views are rare now, but nearby the water behaves like a real mountain stream, at one point cascading in a scenic waterfall.

The hiking has been delightful—two running streams, great views, varied habitats, a sense of wildness. But soon the canyon narrows even more. At one point I have to use a log to make it up through a knot of boulders. Hikers with dogs usually lift them up this part. Above this, the stream vanishes, views are absent, and the canyon, now very narrow, is a jumble of downed trees, broken limbs, and rocks underfoot.

And here is where I first encounter debris from the crash of TWA Flight 260.

At 7:08 a.m. on February 19, 1955, an airport ground-service helper looked up and saw the airplane flying toward the clouds, but instead of flying north as expected, it was flying east-northeast. It was off course—and heading directly toward the mountains. At 7:09, a weather observer saw the plane entering the clouds draped over the mountains.

On the airplane itself, First Officer J. J. Creason prepared the plane for cruising at nine thousand feet, at 230 miles per hour. At 7:12, the terrain-warning bell suddenly sounded. As Charles Williams explained in *The Crash of TWA Flight 260*, the definitive book about the incident, "Instinctively both pilots looked out the window. Nothing but gray cloud, but then, flashing through a weak spot in the cloud just beyond the right wingtip, they saw the sheer cliffside of Sandia Crest—an appalling shock, for they should have been ten miles from the mountain."

Desperately, Captain Spong tried to steer the plane away from the mountain, but hidden by cloud another cliff loomed straight

THE CRASH OF TWA FLIGHT 260

Engine parts from the plane crash in TWA Canyon. Photo by Gerry Sussman.

ahead. "When they struck it, they were still in a left bank, nose high. The plane exploded. The time was 7:13."

Soon, air officials in Albuquerque and Santa Fe became concerned that TWA 260 was overdue and unreported. Efforts to contact the plane received only silence. Something was wrong.

Later that morning, Williams, then an airman stationed at Kirtland Air Force Base, was rock-climbing in the Sandias with a friend. As they started back down the La Luz Trail, they met men with horses and dogs who were searching for a plane believed down in the Sandias. Williams agreed to help them search. By noon, a massive effort had been organized. Hundreds of men and up to fifty airplanes were dispatched to the mountains, but by nightfall they'd found nothing.

Darkness canceled any more searching on Saturday. By Sunday, the crash site had been spotted, but no one yet had reached it.

Early that morning, Williams and several friends arrived at police search headquarters and said they wanted to attempt to reach

CHAPTER ELEVEN

the site from the top. All experienced climbers, they were confident that they could rappel down any cliff in the Sandias.

And sure enough they arrived at the site just as parties from below were arriving. Williams observed the patterns of debris and concluded that the plane had been making a turn when it hit the cliff; it had been heading west, not east.

Williams, who was active at the site throughout the entire recovery operation, recounted in his book the tragic details of the crash scene as well as extensive personal information about the victims, and he was involved with establishing a memorial plaque at the site with relatives and descendants of the victims.

The crash of TWA 260 altered his life.

The Civil Aeronautics Board (CAB) began investigations immediately after the crash. The critical question was, why had Captain Spong steered his craft east instead of west, as he'd done so many times before? Based on evidence far too complex to summarize here, the CAB concluded, "The Board determines that the probable cause of this accident was a lack of conformity with prescribed en route procedures and the deviation from airways at an altitude too low to clear obstructions ahead."

In other words, Spong had screwed up. Pilot error. Some people even speculated that Spong had committed suicide by plane crash, taking fifteen other lives with him.

That was too much for Spong's friends and relatives, who protested. But more important, another TWA pilot, Larry De Celles, thought he knew exactly what had caused the crash: a fluxgate compass. This is a simple electronic device, small coils of wire around a permeable magnetic material, that senses directly the horizontal component of the earth's magnetic field. In the airline industry, it has been used by electronic autopilot for course corrections.

And De Celles knew from personal experience that the units could fail.

Williams tells of the long and determined struggle by De Celles and others to reopen the CAB investigation and perhaps revisit their conclusion. Ultimately they won, and Spong was exonerated. Also, having to confront the fallible fluxgate compass, the airline industry was forced to make changes.

I've seen the wreckage many times; it arouses somber emotions. What I look for now is the memorial plaque placed by the victims' relatives and descendants and others involved in the crash and its aftermath. The memorial has seventeen names: each of the sixteen persons who died in the crash—and the plane itself.

I also look for the silver-colored metal medallion pinned to a tree. It's one of about a hundred similar medallions placed by an unknown person on large trees in the Sandias. Each commemorates an event that occurred the year the tree sprouted. Most are inconspicuous, but the one here is easy to find. It commemorates the crash.

The trail actually continues beyond the crash site to reach the crest, but few hikers do that. The crash site is the destination, almost a pilgrimage.

The hike back always is an anticlimax. The cliff-face views are at my back; the temperature increases as I descend. I'm tired, my heart heavy. I wonder if I'll ever return, but eventually I always do. Maybe I'll just go as far as the waterfall and just hang out there. Or maybe something at the site itself will call to me, and I'll return, perhaps because there's still a message there that I need to hear.

To Learn More

Read *The Crash of TWA Flight 260*, by Charles M. Williams (Albuquerque: University of New Mexico Press, 2010). This is the definitive account of the crash and its aftermath, written by someone who was involved from the very beginning and who has remained involved. It's compelling reading.

CHAPTER TWELVE

The Civilian Conservation Corps in the Sandias

AT 6:00 A.M. the bugle blows, and in your barracks you and about forty-nine other young men tumble out from your steel-framed army-surplus beds, get dressed, make your beds, and then assemble at the parade grounds for muster, watched over by the American flag on a tall flagpole. Then you go to the mess hall for breakfast, grab your equipment, and clamber into a large truck to be taken to the day's operation.

Sounds like wartime, but as you've doubtless guessed, I'm playing off the resemblance to a military operation to describe a different mobilization here in New Mexico, in the Sandia Mountains east of Albuquerque. The youths were enrollees in the Civilian Conservation Corps (CCC), and they had been recruited to combat poverty and unemployment during the Great Depression. It was a bold effort that during the CCC's nine years of existence changed the lives of the three million young men who participated, and changed as well the infrastructure of the states in which they worked.

But now back to you, as a young enrollee from, say, Estancia.

CHAPTER TWELVE

Kiwanis Cabin on the Sandia Crest. Photo by Robert Julyan.

You're eighteen years old, just old enough to meet the minimum age requirement, and you can prove it, unlike many of your friends who lied about their age to be accepted.

You weigh a lean 125 pounds, and because your parents are bean farmers you had no trouble meeting the minimum weight requirement of 107 pounds. You know at least one slightly built youth who on weighing day had chugged water and gorged on bananas to make weight.

Like 81 percent of your fellow enrollees, you have a Hispanic surname. And because you grew up helping on the farm, this will be your first paying job, like two-thirds of the enrollees. The salary will not be much, thirty dollars a month—about a dollar a day for what often will be very hard labor—but you won't see even that, because you're required to send twenty-five of that thirty dollars back to your family.

On the other hand, you will be fed, clothed, and housed, and most important, you will have a job. For this is the Great

THE CIVILIAN CONSERVATION CORPS IN THE SANDIAS

Jaral Canyon work cabin today. Photo by Robert Julyan.

Depression. Even before that event gripped the nation, New Mexico was the country's poorest state, and with the Depression 30 percent of New Mexican youths were unemployed. Thirty dollars with room and board—all across America were millions of able-bodied men who eagerly would have traded places with you.

You've seen them. Blighted souls hopping into empty train boxcars to get down the road, looking for work. You've seen them in rickety jalopies with steaming radiators hoping to make it to the next town before breaking down. You remember seeing a youth about your age knocking at your parents' door, asking for a chore to do in exchange for a bite to eat. You gave what you could, but there really wasn't any work.

No, you feel fortunate indeed as you and your friends hoist your shovels and picks and pile into a truck to begin the long, twisting ride up to the top of the Sandias. As it begins rolling on the approximately twelve-mile dirt road to the crest, you look back at your camp. It has the uninspiring name of F-8-N. The *F* meant

CHAPTER TWELVE

that it operated under the aegis of the US Forest Service, *8* designated it as the eighth camp in the state, and *N* referred to New Mexico. It's located in a pleasant location at 7,100 feet in the area known as Sandia Park. You're fortunate in not being among the first enrollees, as you'd have slept in tents. By the time you arrived they'd been replaced by cabins, albeit nothing fancy; in fact, they were designed to be moved to another location when the work here was completed.

(The camp now is owned by the Boy Scouts, with no public access, although tours by groups may be arranged.)

Now you begin the rough, bumpy ride to Sandia Crest. En route, you'll pass by other CCC projects, either completed or ongoing, including the large, timber picnic shelters at the Doc Long Picnic Area; they'd been built by enrollees living in log cabins in nearby Sulphur Canyon.

Finally, the elevation tops 10,678 feet at Sandia Crest; the truck can go no higher. Today, this is as far as one can drive, but when the CCC was working here a dirt road went to Kiwanis Cabin, so you and your coworkers endure another seven-tenths of a mile before the truck stops. You all pile out, pick up your tools, and get to work. You muscle heavy limestone slabs, locally obtained, into place. At 10,578 feet, only 100 feet lower than the crest, the air is thin, but when your task is done, you'll have helped build a 384-square-foot stone lookout that even more than half a century later, when shorn of its doors and windows and no longer used for organized recreation, remains an enduring landmark in the Sandias, a monument to your resolution and hard work. Not bad for a poor New Mexican boy.

If you've hiked at all in the Sandias, you've been to Kiwanis Cabin. It takes its name from the Albuquerque Kiwanis Club, which erected a log cabin here in the late 1920s. The cabin burned. Then in 1936 the CCC rebuilt it—with stone.

The cabin is reached by a direct, easy, well-marked Forest Service trail from the parking lot below the Crest House. The wooded road goes for a third of a mile before stopping at a log fence demarcating Kiwanis Meadow, a surprisingly large patch of grasses and low, winter-tough shrubs currently closed to the public to protect the vegetation. If you went no further, the hike would have been worth it. You also could reach this point by hiking on a very scenic nature trail along the crest.

Now it's only a short, easy stroll uphill to reach Kiwanis Cabin. It's survived fires, blizzards, ice storms, and if it's lucky it'll survive the human urge to make one's mark. Please don't add more graffiti. So, yes, it is kind of trashed, but it's always a great place for a break or to stop. I've stopped at Kiwanis Cabin countless times in all seasons, but it's always more breathtaking than I remember it, and I always want to stay longer.

And what tales it could tell! From the sweating, cursing, raucous CCC boys to the moonlight picnics with candles. Perhaps rolling out sleeping bags to keep out January cold. Rescuers trying to reach the crash of Flight 260 in TWA Canyon (see chapter 11) would have stopped here. Romantic evenings, desperate evenings, in all kinds of weather. Partying and roasting marshmallows. May it last a thousand years.

CCC camps and projects are everywhere in the Sandias. One of the more conspicuous of them is in Juan Tabo Canyon, the obvious camp-like stone ruins south of Forest Road 333 leading toward Juan Tabo Picnic Area, about 0.75 miles east of Tramway Boulevard. Enrollees here would have worked on projects such as the picnic areas at Juan Tabo and La Cueva, where their stonework remains. The project fit well into the environment and was built to last.

Affiliated with the Juan Tabo barracks would have been the "side camp" or "fly camp" at Jaral Canyon (N 35 12 03 / W 106 26 5.5). Foundations remain, and the spring usually has water. It can be reached from Tramway Boulevard by driving a short distance east to the turnoff for La Cueva Picnic Area, then hiking east to the Tramway Trail, no. 82, and following it south less than half a mile.

CHAPTER TWELVE

Other CCC projects in the Sandias include:

- The Juan Tabo Recreation Area, whose entry gate and large rock shelters exhibit the impressive stonework characteristic of CCC projects.
- The Doc Long Picnic Area and Upper and Lower Sulphur and Cienega Recreation Areas, as well as the Cole Spring and Capulin Recreation Areas.
- Bridges in Las Huertas Canyon and the Las Huertas Recreation Area.
- In fact, if you're hiking and come across stonework, chances are it was made by CCC workers.

The CCC effort lasted only nine years, but the projects they completed endure. Nine years is three times less than I've been going to Kiwanis Cabin. Yet the CCC, along with the Works Project Administration, then as now remain the most popular of President Franklin Roosevelt's New Deal programs. As Richard Melzer said in his book about the CCC in New Mexico, *Coming of Age in the Great Depression*, "From the perspective of six decades or more, former enrollees attest that their CCC experience was not only the key to their coming of age, but also the turning point in their entire lives. Their admiration of the CCC is sincere. The Civilian Conservation Corps is long gone, but its proud legacy endures."

Especially in the Sandias.

To Learn More

Read *Coming of Age in the Great Depression: The Civilian Conservation Corps Experience in New Mexico, 1933–1942*, by Richard Melzer (Las Cruces, NM: Yucca Tree Press, 2000). Melzer's book is a highly readable, comprehensive account of the CCC program throughout New Mexico, with lots of photos and anecdotes.

Read *Field Guide to the Sandia Mountains*, edited by Mary Stuever and Robert Julyan (Albuquerque: Friends of the Sandia Mountains; University of New Mexico Press, 2005). This book has an excellent section about CCC projects in the Sandias.

Read *Sandia Mountain Hiking Guide*, by Mike Coltrin (Albuquerque: University of New Mexico Press, 2005). This is the best hiking guide to the mountains, with lots of information about CCC sites and how to find them.

CHAPTER THIRTEEN

El Cerro de Tomé

IT WAS A cool but sunny Sunday morning in January when I again visited El Cerro de Tomé. I'd driven south from Albuquerque on NM 47 through the eastern part of Los Lunas, then farther south to where Tomé Hill Road headed east to the hill's western base. I then drove 0.75 miles around its southwest side to a parking area at La Puerta del Sol (the Gate of the Sun) sculpture park. Here, Armando Alvarez had created a cast-iron arch framing the hill topped by three crosses, beneath which were cast-iron sculptures of early Spanish explorers and colonizers who passed by the hill on their way north into New Mexico. Interpretive signs around the sculpture park tell their stories.

But, like everyone else, I was there for the hill, so I walked across the road to where the so-called South Trail slabs steeply toward the top. A young man ahead outpaced me, while another passed me from behind. Of El Cerro's two main trails, the half-mile South Trail is the most direct but also the steepest and rockiest, although spur and side trails allow for breaks. I was glad I had brought a walking stick. The one-mile Via Cruces (Crosses Way) from the

CHAPTER THIRTEEN

west is easier but still rocky and sometimes steep. It's the route of most Good Friday pilgrims.

The two young men have descended by the time I reach the top. Far below, a woman has begun her ascent. On top I am alone with the crosses, the hill, the sky, and the silence. Below, the flat and fertile floodplain lies like a vast carpet. Behind rise the Manzano Mountains.

Far to the south, barely visible in the haze, is another volcanic hill, labeled on maps as Black Butte but said to also have a Native American name, El Turututu. I've been to its top and found traces of ancient Indian habitation, just as exist on El Cerro de Tomé. It too is said to have a Native name, recorded as Piu-Whey; others have said that Natives refer to it as "Rabbit Hill." But, as I know well, such prosaic descriptive names often have little correlation with the true significance of the feature in Indian beliefs.

I have climbed El Cerro many times, both at times when people swarm over it like ants on an anthill and at other times when relatively few people are on it (it's all but impossible to be completely alone on the mountain). I recommend both: on Good Friday, to experience the fervent and durable faith of New Mexico's mostly Hispanic Catholics, and at quieter times, to experience for oneself the mountain's potential power.

Yet the story of how El Cerro came to be such a potent symbol of faith is not what many would suspect.

No one knows when humans first worshiped at this volcanic hill extruding from the Rio Grande floodplain. The more than 1,800 petroglyphs now fading on the hill's volcanic boulders and cliffs were pecked as far back as two thousand years ago. Looking closely along the flat stretch along the Via Cruces, about halfway to the top, reveals the low, badly eroded outlines of room blocks and a plaza. Long before the Christian pilgrimages here, the mountain witnessed other religious ceremonies and drumming and dancing.

Then Spanish speakers arrived. Don Juan de Oñate would have

EL CERRO DE TOMÉ

Crosses atop Tomé Hill. Photo by Robert Julyan.

passed near the hill during his 1598 entrada. Skirting the floodplain, the Camino Real (Royal Road) passed just to the east of Tomé Hill. Later, a valley branch ran west of the hill, through Tomé Plaza and then to Isleta Pueblo. Soldiers, settlers, traders, missionaries, hunters, Indian raiders, herders—all passed by the hill.

In 1651 Tomé Domínguez arrived, and ten years later his son, Tomé Domínguez de Mendoza, had established a hacienda nearby. They had barely become established, however, when the Pueblo Revolt erupted in 1680. They fled to Mexico and did not return, although one member of the family did.

But their name remained, on the hill and on the tiny settlement nearby.

As for its religious significance among the local Catholics, I've always wondered if far in the past something happened at the mountain to inspire its sacredness—a miraculous healing, the appearance of a saint or the Virgin. To be sure, crosses and shrines exist atop

CHAPTER THIRTEEN

high points throughout Hispanic New Mexico. Sierra de Cristo Rey just west of El Paso, Texas, also attracts numerous pilgrims, braving heat and bandits to reach the top. And the faithful also trek to the top of Sierra de las Tortugas southeast of Las Cruces.

But none of these approach El Cerro de Tomé in significance, with people clogging the adjacent roads for miles on Good Friday but also making pilgrimages every day of the year, ignoring bad weather as they fulfill their religious vows. Surely the volcanic mound must have been imbued with extraordinary spiritual potency such that even the disabled and the elderly, families with small children, feel called to make their way to the summit.

So I was surprised when Baldwin G. Burr, local historian and secretary of the Historical Society of New Mexico, explained to me the true origins of El Cerro's pilgrimage.

El Cerro had always been regarded as a spiritual focus, but not in any unique way, until a local man, Edwin Berry, fulfilled a vow made during World War II. Berry had been born a Baca, a common surname in the area. (Bacaville is a neighborhood in the town of Belen, south of Albuquerque.) When he moved to Los Angeles, he changed his surname to Berry to avoid anti-Hispanic discrimination; he kept the name Berry when he returned to New Mexico because, he is reported to have said, it was interesting to hear what people said about Hispanics when they didn't know that he was one himself.

Berry had been close boyhood friends with Foch Romero, and World War II found them both fighting in Italy. Romero was killed, and Berry vowed that if he survived he would build a *calvario* atop El Cerro to honor those killed in the war. He returned and kept his promise.

It was a daunting task, one that would test his faith, for not only did he and his friends and family members have to transport concrete up the steep hill, they also had to haul up water. But he persevered, and by 1949 he was leading a procession of people from his church up to his shrine. Before that year, Good Friday had been observed primarily with a pageant in the church.

(above) Edwin Berry, leader in creating the shrine on Tomé Hill. Center for Southwest Research Digital Collections.

(right) Petroglyphs on Tomé Hill. Photo by Robert Julyan.

The procession grew, and grew, and grew until it included not just local churchgoers but also the faithful from throughout south-central New Mexico. On Good Friday, people even walk along the shoulders of Interstate 25.

By the hundreds—no, thousands—they come, for a myriad of personal reasons, and not just on Good Friday but every day of the year, in all weather. Some come in fulfillment of a vow. At least

CHAPTER THIRTEEN

one has been committed to carrying a homemade cross to the top *every day*. Others walk the steep, rocky trail to light votive candles or leave offerings. Some come because their family and friends and neighbors will be here, because it's what their community does. Perhaps some teenagers come to see their boyfriends and girlfriends. Little children trudge the impossibly long and steep paths behind their parents and grandparents; they'll carry the memories of those ascents all their lives, and later they'll bring their own children here, carrying the tradition and the stories forward.

So perhaps I was right all along: something miraculous *did* happen—and is still happening—at El Cerro de Tomé. Even in these most secular of times, when all religious traditions are believed to have originated in the distant past, one man's faith in the mid-twentieth century planted a seed that not only germinated but continues to flourish.

Time for me to leave. The woman who had been working her way up the South Trail is nearing the top. Not wishing to intrude upon her solitude, I begin my descent along the Via Cruces. I meet a man heading for the summit, and two vagrant dogs; their faith apparently was shallow because they turned back before reaching the top.

I reflect upon the uniqueness of Tomé Hill among New Mexico's many historic sites. For one thing, the entire hill, 373 feet high and 1.5 miles long, is on the National Register of Historic Places, the only natural feature listed. For another, among the state's hundreds of hills and mountains, El Cerro is climbed by more people, thousands, than any other, and most of them on just one day—Good Friday.

Sacred site, historic site, archaeological site, geologic site—these abound in New Mexico, but no other single place combines them all with the significance of Tomé Hill.

I'm sorry when I finally reach my car, but I'll be back. I've never been disappointed going up Tomé Hill, and I wasn't today.

EL CERRO DE TOMÉ

In 1968, 47,000 acres of the Town of Tomé Land Grant, including El Cerro, were sold to the Horizon Corporation, an East Coast land-development company. The sale sowed division and bitterness in the community, which has persisted for decades. In November 2013, 188 acres that included the hill were transferred back to the Tomé Land Grant, an event of enormous historic and cultural importance to the community. Honored at the ceremony was Assunta Berry, Edwin's niece. "My uncle [who died in 2000] is happy and smiling down on what a truly amazing thing has happened today. It's just the right thing."

To Learn More

Read *Holy Week in Tomé: A New Mexico Passion Play*, translated by Thomas J. Steele (Santa Fe, NM: Sunstone Press, 1976). This drama, with no identifiable author, has been passed down orally in its original Spanish-language version for more than two hundred years.

Read *El Rio Abajo*, edited by Gilberto Espinosa, Tibo J. Chavez, and Carter M. Waid (Portales, NM: Bishop Publishing, n.d.).

Read *Rio Abajo Heritage* (Los Lunas, NM: Valencia County Historical Society, 1980).

Read *Rio Abajo Prehistory and History of Rio Grande Province*, edited by Michael P. Marshall and Henry J. Walt (Santa Fe: New Mexico Historic Preservation Program, 1984). Technical and scholarly, this book is a rich source of information about this important region.

CHAPTER FOURTEEN

Airplane Beacons
A Pathway through the Sky

Transcontinental flight over western New Mexico, circa 1931:

"This is your captain speaking. We're currently experiencing stormy conditions here over western New Mexico, so please keep your seatbelts fastened. I regret to inform you that because of the weather, we're having difficulty staying on course for Los Angeles. Therefore, we must turn around . . . Excuse me, my copilot is saying something."

Voice in the background: "Yes, I hope so . . . Yes, there it is, I see it."

Pause. "Ladies and gentlemen, I have good news. We've been able to sight Beacon 61, atop Oso Ridge in the Zuni Mountains. We'll be able to continue. Enjoy the flight—but keep your seatbelts fastened."

Today, this fictional conversation would seem bizarre—imagine, navigating a transcontinental flight according to what you can see on the ground—but in 1930, before advanced radar and radio and

CHAPTER FOURTEEN

especially satellite locational systems, seeing a ground beacon could be the difference between life and death.

None realized this more than the developers of the midcontinental airway route used by the fledgling Transcontinental Air Transport (TAT) passenger airline, founded in 1929 by Clement Melville Keys. Commercial aviation was in its infancy. It was only two years earlier that Charles Lindbergh had become an international hero by flying solo across the Atlantic. Lindbergh became the technical adviser for the TAT venture, and he laid out the east–west route, to be marked by beacons, which went operational in July 1929. Under the bold new plan, passengers would fly during the day, then connect with a train through the night. The company boasted that one could go from coast to coast in forty-eight hours.

Less than two months later, disaster struck. On September 3, 1929, a TAT Ford Trimotor with eight people on board went down in a severe thunderstorm traveling west from Albuquerque. It crashed on a ridge high up on 11,301-foot Mount Taylor. Although people soon realized the plane was down, they couldn't find the crash site. Lindbergh himself came out from the East to help with the search. After a few long, agonizing days, the plane was found. The five passengers and three crew members all had perished.

Today, most of us have never heard of the 1929 TAT disaster—I certainly hadn't until a friend told me about it in connection with this project—but in 1929, when transcontinental aviation was just trying its wings, the crash was national news, the first major plane

Transcontinental Air Transport Ford Trimotor plane at the Albuquerque airport during a revisit in the 1960s. Photo courtesy of the Cavalcade of Wings collection.

Restored airway beacon and support buildings at the Aviation Heritage Museum at Grants-Milan Municipal Airport. Photo by Robert Julyan.

crash on a regular commercial land route. It begs comparison with the 1986 space shuttle Challenger disaster. Within five months of the Mount Taylor crash, three other serious airline crashes occurred.

TAT never recovered. The disaster coincided with the Great Depression, and fewer people needed to fly. The company underwent several mergers and eventually merged with Western Air Express to become Trans World Airlines (TWA).

Following the crash, the local economy also was devastated. Among the victims was Amasa McGaffey. He was a lumber magnate and well-connected businessman who drove the economy of much of western New Mexico. A sawmill town in the Zuni Mountains south of Gallup still bears his name. When he died, his energy and drive were gone, and then the Depression arrived.

It was the 1929 New Mexico crash that convinced Lindbergh—and the government—that the route should go farther south to avoid Mount Taylor and straighten the airway. A series of beacon

CHAPTER FOURTEEN

(left) Restored beacon house No. 61 atop Oso Ridge in the Zuni Mountains. Photo by Robert Julyan.

(below) Transcontinental Air Transport Ford Trimotor plane at Oxnard Field in Albuquerque. Photo courtesy of the Cavalcade of Wings collection.

light towers were to be located at high points—ridges, mesas, mountaintops, and other highly visible points—every ten to fifteen miles.

The Civil Aeronautics Administration and the Lighthouse Service had adopted a standard design from the late 1920s: a fifty-one-foot steel tower bearing a one-million-candlepower white beacon, twenty-four inches in diameter. Rotating six times a minute, the thousand-watt flash could be seen for up to forty miles on a clear night. When more powerful thirty-six-inch beacons were deployed, the spacing between towers increased to fifteen miles.

AIRPLANE BEACONS

Two stationary eighteen-inch "on-course" lights also were mounted atop the towers, with either green or red lenses. When a pilot saw a green light, he knew that the beacon was located at or adjacent to an emergency landing strip. At intermediate route beacon sites with no landing strip, the course lights shone red.

Steven Owen, with the Aviation Heritage Museum at Grants-Milan Municipal Airport, points out that, given the smaller size and slower speeds of airplanes then, "you didn't need to have much of an airstrip, you just needed to have the holes filled in."

The colored course lights also flashed in Morse code a letter corresponding to the number of the beacon site along a hundred-mile segment of the airway. They turned on for 0.5 seconds for a dot, 1.5 seconds for a dash. To determine their position, pilots simply had to remember the phrase "When Undertaking Very Hard Routes, Keep Direction by Good Methods," the ten initial letters corresponding to the ten beacon numbers in the hundred-mile segment.

In addition, the beacons sites were designed for daytime navigation; a sixty-five-foot colored arrow, concrete in the early years and later of steel panels, was built at each site.

The beacons originally were designed for pilots in open-cockpit planes (haven't seen them lately at the airport), flying at one thousand feet above the terrain. The lights were aimed slightly upward, to be brightest to an approaching pilot as he overflew the next beacon on the line.

Beside the tower, usually on the tail of the concrete arrow, was a ten-by-fourteen-foot one-room building that housed two 1,500-watt generators as well as switchgear and spare parts. It also gave shelter to the local beacon keeper on his appointed rounds in bad weather. At each tower site, 515-gallon fuel tanks were installed, one for each generator.

Eventually, 1,500 beacons were built around the country, covering eighteen thousand miles of airways. New Mexico was crossed by three: a southern route between San Diego and El Paso; the midcontinental route connecting the coasts; and a north–south route between El Paso and Pueblo, Colorado, through Albuquerque.

CHAPTER FOURTEEN

Beacon 61 high on the Continental Divide was an especially important beacon in this system, partly because of the realignment of the airways after the 1929 TAT crash on Mount Taylor and also because several other planes had gone down along this section of the airway. Bad weather and poor visibility, thin air, and rising slopes were often the lethal factors in crashes on high ridges, or in the lava flow known as El Malpais just to the southeast.

Owen, who along with Dick Cochran began the Aviation Heritage Museum, of which Beacon 61 is a satellite historic site, said, "The Continental Divide is a death trap for pilots." The beacon's location atop Oso Ridge in the Zuni Mountains gave it exceptional visibility to pilots.

So when the airway was shifted away from Mount Taylor in 1931, Beacon 61 was put into operation. It remained in faithful service until 1969.

And in a sense it's still there, although along with other New Mexico beacons it was decommissioned when the Federal Aviation Administration began tracking all air traffic across the country with radar. In 2011 Passport in Time (PIT) volunteers from the US Forest Service's Cibola National Forest Mount Taylor Ranger District stabilized the old generator shed for Beacon 61 crowning Oso Ridge beside the modern fire lookout. Today, what remains of the site shares Oso Ridge with a Cibola National Forest Zuni Mountains Ranger District fire lookout.

Beacon 61 can be reached from either the north or south side of the Continental Divide, which runs along the top of the ridge. Both approaches use Forest Road 50. The southern access begins from NM 53 at the west end of Grants and follows the highway for 17.5 miles. From there it's approximately 1.5 miles over an unpaved but relatively good forest road to its junction with Forest Road 187 leading to the lookout tower.

My preference, however, is to take Forest Road 50, unpaved but good, from the north, starting near the beginning of NM 53. After all, this book is about history, and this route has lots of it.

AIRPLANE BEACONS

After about two miles you enter Zuni Canyon, hemmed by steep sandstone walls. Here you begin noticing the remains of the railroad grade over whose tracks, now gone, trains transported logs to Grants for shipment to mills in Albuquerque. Look at the south walls for signs of the chutes used to get logs from the forests above to the railroad below. Today, the Zuni Mountains are pleasantly forested, but early photographs show them completely denuded, the trees first having gone for railroad ties for the Atchison, Topeka and Santa Fe Railway and mining camp construction in the late 1800s, then later, in the 1920s, to the lumber mills in Albuquerque.

After ten miles, Zuni Canyon opens onto a broad area containing a small lava flow and the site of a logging camp called Malpais Springs, after the springs hidden in the lava. I've searched for the springs four times and found them twice—in different locations.

Forest Road 50 continues through pleasant, forested country, until at N 35 02 41 / W 108 04 59 you reach the turnoff for the one-mile side trip to Paxton Springs, once the headquarters for the Breece logging operations in the Zuni Mountains. George E. Breece was a lumber magnate during this period.

At 8.8 miles from Zuni Canyon you reach the junction with the forest road that leads after 1.5 miles to Forest Road 187. This steep, rocky half-mile road leads to Oso Ridge and the beacon; it's rough and unsuitable for most cars, and if the fire watcher isn't present the gate is locked, so hike the last half mile.

I found the fire watcher thoroughly engaging, and we chatted pleasantly about his solitary working life atop this remote mountain. Of course, he isn't there all the time, and he has an unsurpassed view. Like any job, it has its requirements and routines.

Thanks to the Passport in Time project, volunteers repaired and restored the generator house's exterior at Oso Ridge and installed interpretive signs telling the building's story. It's stabilized for now, until more money is available. The beacon's base concrete slab is still there. And proudly displayed with new orange-and-white paint is the 1931 generator house of Beacon 61.

CHAPTER FOURTEEN

For more than three decades, the airway beacons were important navigational tools that gave a welcome margin of safety for persons traveling the early airways, but their time was ending. Dramatic advances in radio-navigation signal systems, airplane-location instruments, and higher flying elevations (no more open cockpits) eventually made the beacons obsolete. By the mid-1960s, radar, not visual beacons, were tracking aircraft. The last visual airway beacon was shut down in 1973, although a few have continued operating in western Montana. People have forgotten about them. Many, like me, had never heard of them. An important part of American aviation history was being lost.

Or at least it was until 2010, when the Cibola County Historical Society and Passport in Time undertook to preserve that history at an Aviation Heritage Museum located at Grants-Milan Airport. The project features existing and relocated airway beacons, with the buildings to be restored to their original appearance with interpretive signs, relics, maps, and brochures.

The beacons are part of a lost Americana, like gas-station attendants who pumped your gas and washed your windshield. Imagine, flying across country using only your eyes for navigation. Nowadays, much en route navigation is controlled by autopilot, although it's a myth that pilots don't steer anymore; they certainly do during takeoff and landing and during other situations.

But relics of that lost America still exist on the landscape, and in the Zuni Mountains, arguably New Mexico's forgotten mountains, they're especially abundant; old mining camps, old timber camps, old railroad grades, logging chutes, and, atop Oso Ridge, Airway Beacon 61.

A More Accessible Beacon

For years I'd driven NM 41 five miles north from Moriarty to the site of the abandoned homesteader community of Otto (N 35 04 22 / W 106 01 04). A sign had said that it was used as a scientific facility, and everything looked that way. But after seeing the beacon sites

AIRPLANE BEACONS

on Oso Ridge and at Grants-Milan Airport and learning that Otto had also been a beacon site, I realized that was what I had been seeing: the generator house, the tower, and probably the arrow on the ground. I've heard that an emergency airstrip had been at Otto. Suddenly Otto became more interesting.

To Learn More

By all means visit the Aviation Heritage Museum at Grants-Milan Municipal Airport, off the western Interstate 40 frontage road just west of Milan. Look for signs to Airport Road (N 35 10 06 / W 107 53 56.5). There's an exhibit in the airport building itself, as well as the museum in a restored beacon generator house, a work in progress. If you're lucky, someone will be around or can be called to give you a complete tour.

Visit the website www.passportintime.com for the Forest Service's Passport in Time project. Preserving aviation history is ongoing, and it's only one of their goals.

CHAPTER FIFTEEN

Homestead Canyon
Land of Hope and Broken Dreams

I'M HIKING TO an archaeological site in the Cebolla Wilderness, southeast of El Malpais between Pie Town and Grants, going cross-country through an open forest of junipers, piñon, and ponderosa pines. The sandy soil came from of Cebollita Mesa four hundred feet above. It would have been easy for farmers to till the land here—if only there were water. Throughout this area, springs are rare. Game would have been abundant, as it is now—deer, elk, wild turkeys, rabbits—but these people were farmers. How did they live here? How harsh their lives must have been!

It's the same question I've asked at almost every archaeological site I've visited in the Southwest, but this one is different: these people spoke my language, and they've left records of what their lives were like here.

They were homesteaders.

Homesteading. Staking out a plot of government-owned land, 160 acres at first, perhaps more later, building some kind of living quarters, trying to wrestle a subsistence from the tough, harsh

CHAPTER FIFTEEN

The homestead in Homestead Canyon. Photo by Robert Julyan.

land, living there for five years, and, if you were among the most hardy, filing papers saying that you'd "proved up." Then the land was yours.

Homesteading. With the passage of the first Homestead Act in 1862, homesteading altered the land and the culture of America. As much as 10 percent of the US land mass, 270 million acres, was homesteaded; 93 million Americans are descended from homesteaders, many still living on land claimed by their forebears.

Yet despite the TV show *Little House on the Prairie*, homesteading never has been romanticized like herding cattle over long distances or living in a rowdy frontier town. Things were just too difficult. Still, owning your own land, then as now, was part of the American dream, and as long as one could homestead, anyone, even the poorest man, woman, or former slave, if they were tough and persistent enough, could prove up.

Few homesteads in New Mexico survived more than ten years. Most former homesteaders state candidly that the homestead experiment in New Mexico failed. But those years of homesteading were the most challenging, difficult, intense, character-building, and memorable years of their lives. In not one of the memoirs I've read do the homesteaders wish to return to that life. Yet at the same time there's a wistfulness to their recollections, and often nostalgia for the good times that went alongside the bad.

And while the people are gone, their homesteads remain, poignant reminders of the lives they led, the dreams they attempted. I'm headed now to one of their cabins in the appropriately named Homestead Canyon.

I've lost my trail among a maze of cow paths as I enter a broad valley about a mile east of the trailhead, itself about a mile east of the so-called Pie Town Road. No problem; I have a map, and even better I have a GPS unit and GPS coordinates to the site (N 34 40 50 / W 107 56 52). I wish I could enthuse about the scenery, but I

The fate of all log homesteads. Photo by Robert Julyan.

CHAPTER FIFTEEN

The remains of an automobile. Photo by Robert Julyan.

can't; this land has been used—and used hard. Sawed stumps, cattle trails, scraps of lumber and tin, severe overgrazing. As I hike I see a small Puebloan site, just a small mound of stones. Long before ranchers and homesteaders and lumbermen arrived, other people were here using the land. Black-on-white pottery suggests that they were here in Chacoan times.

The first time I came to these Cebolla Wilderness canyons, a rancher bearded me to complain about how "this ain't wilderness." In a sense he was right; the 1964 Wilderness Act defined *wilderness* as "earth and its community of life untrammeled by man, where man himself is a visitor who does not remain," but regrettably this land has been soundly trammeled. But, I thought, in a hundred years it could be much less so. If overgrazing can be controlled—grazing is allowed now as a preexisting use of the wilderness—grasses would return, the water table would rise, erosion would subside, and wildlife would increase. Actually, to the animals here it already *is* wilderness. On this trip and one to Armijo Canyon a few days later I saw tracks of elk, deer, rabbits, coyotes, foxes, even a mountain lion—and a live bear. If only there were water . . .

The terrain in Homestead Canyon is easy and open. Rather than look for *the* trail, I use my GPS to go cross-country. As I ascend a gentle slope, I notice potsherds that have washed down from higher ground. I remember from earlier hikes in the area that potsherds are *everywhere*.

HOMESTEAD CANYON

I had to wonder what the newly arrived homesteaders thought when they saw on the land reminders of earlier peoples who also had attempted farming here: abandoned pueblos and field houses, broken pottery, manos and metates, flakes of chert. These Puebloans, whose descendants still live at the modern pueblos of Zuni, Acoma, and Laguna, had built shelters, turned the soil with digging sticks, planted crops, prayed for rain—then departed.

I see more broken pottery as I descend a long slope, and then I notice a scatter of rusted tin cans, old pails, scraps of wood, broken modern pottery. A few decades from now we might call it a midden heap; now it's a trash pile.

The homesteader debris atop the ancient pottery is no surprise. For as long as people have settled New Mexico they've built upon the same sites as people before them: springs, streams, places with good soil or rainfall, preferred areas for game. To find the stones the Indians used to build their dwellings, look in the stone walls of the homesteads.

The eponymous homestead of Homestead Canyon was no primitive hovel but rather a log cabin of substantial ponderosa pine logs. The main building had three rooms, but curiously no interior door connected them; instead, they had three separate exterior doors. Jennifer (Schramm) Cutillo, a park ranger with the Bureau of Land Management's Grants Field Station office, said that it reminded her of a motel.

Nearby is a substantial root cellar, standard for most homesteads. One homesteader woman said that it was not uncommon to can one thousand jars preparing for the long winter. Also nearby are a barn, a corral, and an outhouse. Down the slope from the house are the scavenged remains of a vehicle.

I step inside one of the rooms and try to imagine what the homesteader would have seen from the window: fields plowed by hand or with a horse; a rough two-track leading to the house; sandstone cliffs; ponderosas and piñons, both essential for subsistence here. As I gazed, I imagined the homesteader and his family looking out

CHAPTER FIFTEEN

on the November day in 1931 when the Big Storm struck, dumping five feet of snow, killing livestock, and forcing the people to subsist on bread, gravy, and game such as jackrabbits and porcupines. They shared these and other hardships with their Navajo neighbors at the Ramah Navajo Indian Reservation.

Who were these homesteaders? All I've learned about the ones who lived in Homestead Canyon is that a 1989 archaeological survey found a 1931 Texas license plate; that fits with the time and origin of most homesteaders.

Without doubt people were filing homestead claims in New Mexico as soon as the act was passed in 1862, but homesteading here mainly occurred in two main waves. The first was around 1900, when a wet phase in the climate coincided with the completion of railroads. Promotional materials back east lured hundreds of farmers to New Mexico's eastern plains. Advertising images from the time showed steamboats on Missouri-sized rivers near the town of Logan in the far eastern part of the region. The hopeful farmers established scores of communities, with stores and post offices and schools and churches, communities such as Hollene, Ima, Macy, Broadview, Field, Claud, Allie, Belcher, Benson, and scores more. When dry conditions returned, as they always do, the homesteaders departed, leaving behind ranches and farm towns dead or dying.

Then beginning around 1929, as farmers were leaving the eastern plains, another homesteading wave occurred. People often assume that these homesteaders were refugees from the Dust Bowl, but while many were indeed from the southern Great Plains, they were not part of that exodus. Many were World War I veterans. As Sherry Robinson said in her guide to west-central New Mexico, *El Malpais, Mt. Taylor, and the Zuni Mountains*, "These were not the Joads."

The greatest challenge faced by most homesteaders was obtaining water, unless they were fortunate in having a spring nearby, as did Diego Armijo at his homestead in Armijo Canyon, just south of Homestead Canyon. This homestead (N 34 39 27 / W 107 56 02) is very different from its neighbor in Homestead Canyon. It was

Dugout home of Faro and Doris Caudill. Pie Town, New Mexico, June 1940. Courtesy of the Library of Congress, Prints and Photographs Division, LC-USF34-036584-D [P&P]. Lee, Russell, 1903–1986, photographer.

The homesteading Caudill family, from left: Josie, Doris, and Faro. Courtesy of the Library of Congress, Prints and Photographs Division, LC-USF34-036560-D [P&P]. Lee, Russell, 1903–1986, photographer.

constructed with a mix of techniques—adobe, horizontal logs, vertical poles—with a stone chimney. It had a cement floor. But most importantly, it had a water source, Armijo Spring, just uphill.

I wondered how the homesteaders in Homestead Canyon got their water; there was no spring, the drainage in the valley was intermittent at best, and I saw no evidence of a well, although that would have been easy to overlook. No wonder the Armijo Canyon homesteaders built a small shrine in the grotto protecting their spring, but when I was there in the summer of 2013, the spring was dry. When I approached the spring, a small bear scurried away. Where would it get water?

And what of the deer and elk and coyotes and foxes and even the mountain lion whose tracks I saw?

CHAPTER FIFTEEN

Probably the best portrait of these homesteaders can be found in Joan Myers's book *Pie Town Woman*. She tells the story of Doris Caudill, who came to a homestead eleven miles south of Pie Town, married a local man, had a daughter, and stuck it out for ten hard years. The book also features the photographs of Russell Lee, one of the best-known Depression-era photographers; he worked for the federal Farm Service Agency, which disseminated his photographs nationwide. Lee arrived in Pie Town in April 1940 with his wife, Jean, stayed for six weeks, and took more than six hundred black-and-white photographs, many of which appeared in magazines such as *LIFE*. About one hundred of the photos were of Doris Caudill, her husband, Faro, and their daughter, Josie.

The Caudills' homesteads (Faro's father lived nearby) differed from those in Homestead and Armijo Canyons in being dugouts, built partly underground. Such houses were easier to heat in winter. Most floors were dirt anyway, even in aboveground structures. Newspapers served as wallpaper, pasted up so that visitors could read them. On the walls of the Caudill dugout was a luxury lacking in most homesteads—a mirror.

As for water, most homesteaders such as the Caudills dug wells by hand, hauled water, or prayed for rain. Until they dug a well, the Caudills hauled water. As Joan Myers described the routine:

> Faro had to go down to Pop's, borrow a team of horses, then walk up to Aunt Lizzie's and borrow a wagon, and drive five or six miles past their neighbor Granny Johnson's place, almost halfway to the highway. At the windmill there, he would use buckets to fill the containers on the wagon. He then brought the water home, returned the wagon to his aunt and the horses to his father, and walked home. He would do that twice a week.

Despite isolation almost unthinkable today, the Caudills nonetheless got together from time to time with neighbors. They lived in a diffuse community about eleven miles south of Pie Town called Divide, because it was near the Continental Divide.

There were church activities, celebrations such as weddings and birthdays, farm association meetings, and other community get-togethers. Doris Caudill was active in the local literary society. She remembers fondly going with friends into El Malpais to a lava cave with permanent ice and bringing back enough to make ice cream.

They made shopping trips to Pie Town and Grants, although they rarely bought more than coffee, flour, and sugar. The flour sacks became clothing.

By the time Russell Lee was taking photographs around Pie Town, the way of life he was recording was ending. The Depression was waning, and World War II with abundant war-related employment was imminent. By 1940 most homesteaders had concluded that subsistence farming on a couple hundred arid acres in central New Mexico was not really viable. For about ten years they'd given it their best shot, and they had very little to show for it. Lee's wife, Jean, later recalled, "We knew these people probably couldn't make it. That land never should have been stirred with a stick. There was no good topsoil, none at all."

In 1942 Doris Caudill acceded to Faro's desire to move to Albuquerque and a paying job. They both found work, but the marriage that had survived the hardships of homesteading failed in prosperity. After they divorced, Doris eventually moved to Alaska—and more homesteading. There she remarried, and she and her new husband eventually settled near the mouth of the Columbia River in Oregon, one of the nation's wettest places.

A few homesteaders stuck it out, perhaps because they'd grown accustomed to the life, perhaps out of sheer cussedness.

As I walked around the homestead in Homestead Canyon, I realized that less than one hundred years had passed since someone had lived there, and already everything was falling into ruin. The roofs were collapsing into the house and the root cellar, the timbers were decaying. In another one hundred years the timbers

CHAPTER FIFTEEN

would be gone, the tin cans and pails and hinges and wood stoves would have rusted away, and all that would remain would be vague depressions from cellar holes, stones and rubble outlining building foundations, and broken crockery. In other words, they'd be all but indistinguishable from the ancient Indian ruins in the area.

Trying to wrest a living from this harsh land is an old, old story.

The Cerro Montoso Homesteaders

About the same time that Doris and Faro and Josie and their neighbors were scrabbling to survive around Pie Town, another group of Anglo homesteaders had moved onto previously uninhabited land west of the Rio Grande near Cerro Montoso northwest of Taos. Local Hispanics had never settled there because the area lacked water; they called it La Otra Banda (the Other Side) but the homesteaders gave it a try, and soon local Hispanics were filing claims, so as not to be left out. Relations between the two groups were often strained.

If anything, the land here was even less suited for farming than that near Pie Town, but the homesteaders here had one great advantage: Prohibition. Making moonshine and bootlegging could be very profitable, especially with Colorado so near. When Prohibition was repealed in 1933, the community's days were numbered, and by the 1940s La Otra Banda was uninhabited once more.

The End of Homesteading

Despite the enormous numbers involved—21 million acres and millions of people—homesteading was an experiment, and in many areas, especially in the West, it failed. The original 160 acres was far too little in the arid west—John Wesley Powell estimated that more than 2,000 acres should be a minimum allotment for a family—and even when the acreage was increased in 1934 with the Taylor Grazing Act to 640 acres, it was still too little. Only when family members filed adjoining claims or bought abandoned allotments were they able to succeed—as ranches, not farms.

In New Mexico, most homesteaders in the 1930s rarely lasted more than ten years; with World War II and the availability of paying jobs elsewhere, most left.

Eventually available land ran out, and many homesteaders were stuck on land patently unsuitable for farming. To address this, Congress in 1937 passed the Bankhead-Jones Farm Tenant Act, which authorized the government to buy back homestead land and give the homesteaders a stake with which to start again elsewhere.

The last woman to file a homestead claim did so in 1984, the last man in 1988—both in Alaska—but the dream of being self-sufficient on land of one's own lives on.

Respect the Past

Although most abandoned homesteads might appear as just crumbling old houses with yards full of junk, they are just as much archaeological sites as ancient cliff dwellings are and should be treated as such. In fact, in a couple hundred years you wouldn't notice much difference on the ground. Therefore, look around the homestead and take photos, but leave everything as you found it. You'd be amazed by what trained archaeologists can learn from the placement of objects on the ground.

To Learn More

Read Sherry Robinson's *El Malpais, Mt. Taylor, and the Zuni Mountains: A Hiking Guide and History* (Albuquerque: University of New Mexico Press, 1994). Her chapter about homesteaders is both moving and informative.

Read Joan Myers's *Pie Town Woman: The Hard Life and Good Times of a New Mexico Homesteader* (Albuquerque: University of New Mexico Press, 2001). This is the best account of homesteader

CHAPTER FIFTEEN

life in central New Mexico. It includes Russell Lee's photographs and Myers's interviews with Doris Caudill and other surviving homesteaders.

Because much if not most homesteading in the West was on land now administered by the US Bureau of Land Management (BLM), including the Homestead Canyon and Armijo Canyon homesteads, the BLM has created several excellent websites detailing the history and culture of homesteading. These websites include text, photos, oral histories, and interviews with historians.

CHAPTER SIXTEEN

Smokey Bear

America's Favorite Celebrity

GOOD OLD SMOKEY. Everyone loves Smokey. A few years ago a poll showed Smokey to be the world's most recognizable figure after Mickey Mouse, known in every country; lately Mickey has faded somewhat, yet Smokey endures. While he was alive at the National Zoo in Washington, DC, he received so much mail that he was given his own zip code. That was discontinued after Smokey and his son died, but it's been reinstated. Generations have grown up with Smokey—and continue to do so, even though there hasn't been a living, in-the-fur Smokey Bear since 1991. That's when Smokey's son died. The original Smokey died in 1976 and is entombed in Capitan, New Mexico. Smokey has three hundred thousand likes on Facebook, and twenty-four thousand people follow him on Twitter.

So despite the absence of a live bear, Smokey remains as ubiquitous and popular as ever. Recently, as I was driving east on Interstate 40 in Albuquerque, there, amid the casino and tort attorney billboards, was a billboard bearing Smokey's avuncular image,

CHAPTER SIXTEEN

The roadside vista Smokey with Capitan Gap over his shoulder, where the burned bear cub who became Smokey was found in a tree during a fire in 1950. Photo by Robert Julyan.

looking at me with wise, kind eyes, reminding me that only *I* can prevent wildfires. Smokey lives on, as he should.

That's because Smokey was always more myth than mammal. Most people don't realize that the nation had a Smokey Bear for six years before the little singed bear cub was found clinging to an aspen tree as a forest fire raged in the Capitan Mountains. During World War II, Forest Service officials feared that our enemies would take advantage of the paucity of firefighters who'd become soldiers, so the Wartime Advertising Council, as one of its first campaigns, created Smokey in 1944 as a fictional bear warning people against forest fires. (In fact, the Japanese did launch several firebombing balloons in the jet stream hoping to destroy American forests.)

But the posters and images couldn't compete with the real-life bathos of the little cub, so in a stroke of marketing genius the burned cub assumed the identity of Smokey, and the legend was born.

Almost everyone is familiar with the story. The weather in the Capitan Mountains in south-central New Mexico had been dry, as usual, when on May 4, 1950, a camp stove overheated and began throwing sparks in the Capitan Gap area. Actually, two fires were ignited that day, but they soon combined. A firestorm exploded that jumped a firebreak, trapping twenty-four firefighters, who survived only by burying themselves in recently dug trenches and a recent landslide.

The fire was not controlled for several days. On May 9, firefighters reported several sightings of a small bear cub running around. They mentioned it among themselves. Then they found the cub, its paws and hind legs burned, clinging to an aspen tree in a rock glacier (see page 133). His mother was nowhere to be seen. Had he been the weakest member of a triplet? Or had he been separated from his family during the fire?

Initially the firefighters debated whether to rescue the cub or let nature takes its course, but softer hearts prevailed, and the cub was brought back to camp. The firefighters nicknamed him Hot Foot Teddy. Homer C. Pickens, assistant director of the New Mexico Department of Game and Fish, kept the cub at his home, then Ray Bell, a ranger with the same department, took him to Santa Fe, where he, his wife Ruth, and their children Don and Judy cared for the cub.

Soon the heartwarming story of the little burned bear reached New Mexico game commissioner Elliott Barker, and he saw a signal opportunity to promote forest-fire prevention. He visited Smokey, as the bear had become known, and together with his friend, the Santa Fe photographer Harold Walter (see chapter 1), he spread the story through magazines and other media outlets nationwide. Smokey was flown in a Piper Cub airplane to the National Zoo in Washington, DC, and during an overnight fuel stop in Saint Louis en route a special room was prepared for him at the zoo there. He was greeted at the National Zoo by several hundred spectators, including Boy Scouts, Girl Scouts, photographers, and media. The little bear had captured the country's imagination, and thus the legend of Smokey was born.

CHAPTER SIXTEEN

A child of the fifties, I grew up with Smokey. He was an icon of my youth, like Howdy Doody, but while my friends and I might make fun of Howdy, never Smokey. He was among the few cultural symbols that were universally good; in a confusing and changing world, there was always good old Smokey.

His image was especially visible around Rocky Mountain National Park in Colorado, near where I'd grown up. Until fire suppression began there when the park was established in 1915, enormous fires ravaged the park's forests, and visitors always stopped to take photos of the strange, barren landscape of burned and dead trees.

I've seen several forest fires, and the aftermath always gets uglier the closer you look. But there's a durability to the devastation of a major hot fire that puts it into a different ecological category. In Rocky Mountain National Park, the dead trees are still there, and in Capitan Gap, the site of the fire that singed Smokey, it's hard to believe the forest is still so desolate more than sixty-five years after the event. Dead trees and barren soil are everywhere. It's as if Dresden and Hiroshima never rebuilt after World War II.

I was to find out how charnel the fire had left the mountains when I set out to go to where Smokey had been found. Or more precisely, approximately where he had been found, because it turns out that no one knows the exact location.

When my wife, Mary, and I asked at the Smokey Bear Museum and Visitors' Center in Capitan, no one knew exactly where Smokey had been found, but they referred us to a retired forest ranger who said that Smokey was found about a third of the way down Minckey Ridge. The people at the gift shop said that a marker had been erected at the site, and later some forest rangers searched for it unsuccessfully, but the retired forest ranger said that the marker had been intended but was never put in place.

On my next trip I drove to Ruidoso and the Smokey Bear Ranger District. It turned out that the relatively new district ranger there was David Warnack, whom I'd known and liked from our days in the Gila National Forest working on the Continental Divide Trail.

(above) Firefighters mopping up after the Capitan Gap fire of 1950. Courtesy of the Palace of the Governors Photo Archives, 029671.

(right) The bear cub who became Smokey clinging to an aspen tree on Minckey Ridge. Courtesy of the Palace of the Governors Photo Archives, 128729.

Soon after Warnack arrived in the White Mountains to become district ranger, he organized a search for the Smokey site as a team-building project. He confirmed that Minckey Ridge was indeed the right location, as was the aspen grove in the rock glacier. "We had a guy who somewhat recalled seeing an old metal plaque," Warnack said.

CHAPTER SIXTEEN

"Everybody was very excited, because Smokey Bear is a big part of this ranger district—and a big source of pride. In this community, and in this ranger district, he's an important part of the community's identity. Even at events where the Forest Service is criticized, whenever Smokey comes out he gets big applause."

Actually, Warnack said, among Smokey's few detractors are those claiming that he did his job too well. Since even before Smokey, national forests had been managed under a fire-suppression policy for which Smokey later created massive popular support. Thus, in the absence of small natural burns, part of the natural pruning cycle, many forests became clogged with fuel for a catastrophic fire, should one get started.

And, inevitability, catastrophic fires have occurred. The most famous example was in Yellowstone National Park (mostly in Wyoming), where fire suppression definitely had been the policy until 1972. After then, Yellowstone was managed under a policy of letting small, natural fires burn themselves out. The year 1988 arrived as the driest summer on record. As Lee Whittlesey, the park's historian, told me while on a tour, the major issue was that all those decades with fire suppression left the forests severely overgrown, filled with fuel wood. The result was a fire that summer that left 1.2 million acres scorched and 793,000 acres burned, 36 percent of the park's total acreage. Surveys found that 345 elk (out of more than 30,000), 36 deer, 12 moose, 9 bison, and 6 black bears died in the fire.

So was this Smokey's fault?

Warnack rejects that conclusion. "Smokey didn't say anything about fire management. His message to visitors was, 'Don't *you* start a fire.' He stressed personal accountability. *No fires* was not his message."

The Smokey Bear Ranger District team didn't find the Smokey memorial. "I found a cowbell, though," chuckled Warnack. He did advise that I'd best approach Minckey Ridge from below rather than from above, as I'd planned.

More than sixty-five years later, the slopes of Capitan Gap in the Capitan Mountains still bear the scars of the fire that scarred Smokey. Photo by Robert Julyan.

So I returned to the area to try my hand at finding the elusive marker. After driving over good, then bad, then terrible dirt roads, I pointed my car downslope, locked it, took a GPS way point, and started walking up Minckey Ridge, cross-country, following my GPS. I doubted I'd actually find the marker—likely because it doesn't exist, as the retired forest ranger had claimed—but since when does that stop a true treasure hunter? I promised Warnack that I'd record GPS coordinates if I found it, and take pictures.

No trail, just going straight uphill for what my GPS said would be only 1.5 to 2.0 miles. I like hiking cross-country. I noticed that I had great views.

That, I soon realized, was because this slope had been scoured by fire. No living standing trees. A nightmare of charred and fallen trunks, limbs, branches, many rotten. The few dead trees

CHAPTER SIXTEEN

still standing looked grotesque, like figures from the *Night on Bald Mountain* sequence of Disney's *Fantasia*. Underfoot are pale-brown rocks, many of which appeared to have been spalled by extreme heat. Everything is brown in this drought year. Everything designed to trip me up. Nothing stable. Haring back and forth, seeking unobstructed routes. Failing. Plodding on. According to my GPS, I'd gone less than halfway.

No insects, no deer scat, no scat of any kind, no birds. A dead land. Throw in a few active volcanoes and some sky effects, and this could be Mordor.

This was the land Smokey would have inherited had he not been rescued. Three square meals at Washington's National Zoo and no dangers probably looked good to him. I thought about what Pi, the son of a zookeeper in India and the main character in Yann Martel's novel *Life of Pi*, said of captive zoo animals. Contrary to what humans usually believe, most zoo animals are quite content to live in a cage, growing fat and old without ever worrying about starving, getting hurt, getting killed by a predator or in an accident or any of the million other things that harm animals in the wild. At the zoo, Smokey *subsisted* on a diet of bluefish and trout—along with his favorite, peanut butter sandwiches. He had his own pool. He even had a love life. And countless admirers. Getting stranded in a tree up here on this miserable dry ridge probably was the best thing that ever happened to him. The average life-span of a black bear in the wild is twenty years; Smokey lived to twenty-six at the National Zoo.

I soldiered on. Only a few days earlier I'd hiked to the top of Hermit Peak near Las Vegas, New Mexico. The trail there was long and conspicuously rocky, but it was a stroll over a golf course compared to this.

At a little over a mile I stopped. I was on a long, relatively level stretch of Minckey Ridge, which, thanks to the fire, again gave me expansive views of the mountains. Ahead, the ridge rose higher. And there were the aspen groves amid the rock glaciers. Up there somewhere could be the Lost Smokey Memorial. Humans have sought less valuable treasures. Perhaps someone, someday, will find it.

But not me. For all I knew, I was already close to where Smokey had been found. I took some photos of the rock glaciers and the upper slopes, of the hiking terrain I'd struggled through.

I sat, my back against a charred dead tree, my legs extended onto dry straw-colored grass, tan rocks, and dusty dark soil mostly composed of ash. How long will it take before the mountain revegetates? Not in my lifetime, based on present conditions sixty-five years after the fire. I ate what passed for a lunch and gazed upward. In another time, with more moisture, more plants, this could be beautiful. Even now, with the rock glaciers draping down the slopes, with dramatic rock outcroppings, with the spruce-fir forest on the upper slopes, it had the wild beauty that all truly natural places have.

Few people come here. Hunters in season, but certainly no fishermen. No skiers either. Hikers? A handful, perhaps. The hike to Capitan Peak over a good, well-marked trail is scenic and interesting, but hikers don't pass up the White Mountains or the Gila country to hike in the Capitans.

Interesting, even beautiful country—if you have the luxury of sitting and observing it rather than trying to hike through it. I sat a few minutes more, then headed back.

I tried to find an easier route but didn't succeed. And, while thrashing around in the brush, I allowed the brush to pluck my camera from its case. Discovering that was a bummer yet to come.

At the head of Minckey Canyon, several rock glaciers converged. Dropping into Dry Canyon and hoping to find a trace of a trail, I soon realized that even the streams had been scourged. Nothing had flowed here in a long time; the stream bed was a tangle of fire debris. No trail.

Eventually I encountered the road and hiked the fifth of a mile back to my car.

CHAPTER SIXTEEN

Then, driving out and seeing a particularly revealing view of the burned area, I discovered that the mountains had taken my camera. But none of this was Smokey's fault, and when I drove into Capitan, to the Smokey Bear Café, the Smokey Bear Motel, the Smokey Bear Museum, past the ubiquitous statues and paintings of Smokey, and even more when I saw Smokey's face on a billboard on Interstate 40 in Albuquerque, I realized that it's okay to have Smokey now be a marketing creation, because there once was a real Smokey, caught in a real forest fire, in the Capitan Mountains. And after seeing firsthand a forest that had burned sixty-five years earlier, I approve of his message all the more. Agency officials and foresters and scientists and land managers can recite the latest policies and studies about the wisdom of letting fires burn in the wilderness, but when Smokey talks, America listens.

Not Just Forest Fires

The next time you see a Smokey sign, look closely at his message: it's no longer, "Only you can prevent forest fires"; it's now, "Only you can prevent wildfires"—to include grasslands.

Smokey Bear versus Smokey the Bear

To set the record straight, Smokey's official name is Smokey Bear, despite the fact that most people probably call him Smokey *the* Bear. Much of the confusion results from the 1952 song by Steve Nelson and Jack Rollins, "Smokey the Bear." The songwriters said that they added the "the" to Smokey's name to keep the song's rhythm. The song's chorus is

> *Smokey the Bear, Smokey the Bear.*
> *Prowlin' and a growlin' and a sniffin' the air.*
> *He can find a fire before it starts to flame.*

SMOKEY BEAR

That's why they call him Smokey,
That was how he got his name.

In the 1950s that variant of the name became widespread both in popular speech and in print, including in at least one standard encyclopedia. A 1955 book in the Little Golden Books series published by Western Publishing was titled *Smokey the Bear*, and Smokey calls himself by this name in the book. An easy way to remember the correct form is to recall that we don't say Santa the Claus or Peter the Rabbit. Also, from the beginning, Smokey's name was intentionally spelled differently from the adjective *smoky*.

What Are Rock Glaciers?

During the Pleistocene Epoch (better known as the Ice Age), between 2,588,000 to 11,700 years ago, the great continental glaciers never touched New Mexico. Nonetheless, many mountains here had local glaciers flowing down valleys. In fact, the southernmost glaciation in what is now the United States occurred in New Mexico, on the northeast slope of Sierra Blanca.

In most southern New Mexico mountains, however, the snow never became deep enough to form typical glaciers. Instead, snow and ice accumulated among the rocks on the mountains' slopes, and then the accumulation—the rocks in a matrix of ice—flowed as a unit downhill, as slowly and inexorably as a glacier. After the Pleistocene, when the ice melted, the rocks stayed in place. One way to detect a rock glacier is by the lichens on its rocks. The presence of dense lichen colonies, which grow extremely slowly, means that the rocks have been in place a very long time. Active talus slopes, however, are caused by rockfall from above and haven't been lichenated as long. For those who appreciate such things, the rock glaciers in the Capitan Mountains are magnificent examples of this phenomenon.

CHAPTER SIXTEEN

To Learn More

Visit Smokey Bear State Park and its museum in Capitan. Talk to people there. Smokey owns the town.

Read *Smokey Bear 20252: A Biography*, by William Clifford Lawter Jr. (Alexandria, VA: Lindsay Smith, 1994). This presents the complete story of Smokey in a very readable narrative.

CHAPTER SEVENTEEN

John Tunstall's Murder

The Shot Heard 'Round Lincoln County

PERHAPS THE LINCOLN COUNTY WAR was not technically a war, but to the friends and relatives of those whose lives were lost or ruined, it was a good facsimile. When the three-year conflict finally ended in 1881, the region had been torn apart, dozens of people had died, and seeds of bitterness had been sown that persist to this day. It was a war without winners, thoroughly unnecessary, driven by the worst passions of the Old West, played out by some of the era's worst characters.

And it all began here, on February 18, 1878, on this remote, inconspicuous patch of mountainous forest land. A plaque set in the ground and a marker set in concrete, originally located in 1927 by M. J. Fulton and T. T. Behrens, mark the exact spot where John Henry Tunstall was murdered.

Tunstall was an Englishman born into wealth and privilege. As a young man he made the "Grand Tour" of Europe expected of such a youth, but rather than settling in to work for his father he instead traveled to North America, specifically to Vancouver, British Columbia, where his father had business interests. Again, however,

CHAPTER SEVENTEEN

John Tunstall. Courtesy of the Palace of the Governors Photo Archives (NMHM/DCA), negative 000-742-0151.

he preferred independence, so he traveled around the West seeking opportunities in the sheep-raising industry, which he believed held promise of independent wealth. New Mexico was a center of the sheep industry, so he washed up in Santa Fe. There, he learned that the best sheep land was in the northern and central parts of the state and was already taken. And there he met Alexander McSween, lawyer and promoter, who convinced him that better opportunities existed in cattle raising in southern New Mexico, so he bought a horse and a dog and set out to join McSween in Lincoln County. He was twenty-three.

He bought a ranch on the Rio Feliz, and with McSween as his associate he operated stores and businesses in the frontier town of Lincoln. That set up the conflict, for suddenly the despised monopoly of L. G. Murphy and Company in Lincoln faced competition.

Lawrence Gustav Murphy was an Irish American soldier who during the Civil War had been a sutler at nearby Fort Stanton.

JOHN TUNSTALL'S MURDER

When the Civil War ended, he formed an association with other former soldiers to create L. G. Murphy and Company to supply the fort and also the Mescalero Apaches for whom the fort was responsible. Murphy's business partners included Emil Fritz, at one time the post commander at Fort Stanton; John Riley, another former Fort Stanton officer and fellow Irish American; and James Dolan, a Fort Stanton enlisted man and yet another Irish American. Their various roles in the company differed, as did their personalities. Murphy, on whom the company centered, was described as a natty dresser, convivial, a hale-fellow-well-met, and a heavy drinker with a quick temper.

In 1868 as a post trader he established a substantial store at the fort, but soon Murphy's company was known for the shameful irregularities common among other military post traders throughout the West: overestimating rations distributed to the Indians and submitting false invoices, supplying inferior goods and food, and selling alcohol, which was prohibited. In 1873 Murphy's company was ordered to quit the fort, under military escort if necessary. Murphy and his associates moved to the town of Lincoln, where they established a mercantile business known locally as the House.

Fritz, in poor health, departed in 1873 and died in 1874. That left Murphy, Dolan, and Riley running the business, but as always it was complicated; at one time even McSween worked with the group, and the politician and manipulator Thomas B. Catron, head of the Santa Fe Ring (a notorious group of attorneys and land speculators), became involved, as did the cattle baron John Chisum.

Tunstall arrived in Lincoln County in 1875. As an Englishman, he could not purchase land directly from the US government, so he likely used the common stratagem of financing Americans to buy land, which he then purchased from them. He's said to have had two ranches, one on the Rio Feliz and the other on the Rio Peñasco.

At the same time, Tunstall formed an association—not a partnership—with McSween in forming businesses in Lincoln that competed with the House. Dolan, who ran things during

CHAPTER SEVENTEEN

Murphy's frequent spells of intoxication, was furious. The legal and other machinations that followed are too complex for the purposes of this book; in brief, at one point Dolan tried to get McSween arrested, but McSween escaped to Chisum's ranch, so Dolan got a writ attaching Tunstall's property, believing that that would strike at McSween. A deputy sheriff and posse were dispatched to Tunstall's Rio Feliz ranch. This set in motion the events leading to Tunstall's murder.

David M. Marusa, in his superbly researched history (not yet published) of the Lincoln County War, has synthesized the several accounts of the event, including those by Pat Garrett, George Coe, and others directly or indirectly involved, and while the accounts differ in their details they all paint the same general picture.

Around 8:30 a.m. on February 18, 1878, a chilly morning but nonetheless auguring a pleasant day, Tunstall and four cowboys set out from the Rio Feliz to drive a small herd of horses, fewer than ten, to Lincoln, perhaps to settle the judgment, perhaps to hide them. The cowboys were Dick Brewer, Robert Widenmann, John Middleton, and William Bonney, better known as Billy the Kid.

The route they followed was over low, gentle hills, forested and brushy, and as evening approached they were at the head of a small canyon that ultimately would join the valley of the Rio Hondo. They were making good time and had covered perhaps fifty to sixty miles.

The posse pursuing them was making even better time. They'd gone to Tunstall's Rio Feliz ranch. There they split up, a subposse led by William Morton following Tunstall more aggressively.

As Tunstall's party began to descend the valley at the head of what is now called Tunstall Canyon, they spotted wild turkeys, and eating one for supper sounded good, so the cowboys took after them, leaving Tunstall alone and unprotected.

What happened when the posse came upon Tunstall can never be known. Morton claimed that Tunstall fired first and the posse shot Tunstall in self-defense, but few people give credence to that story. For one thing, Tunstall rarely carried a gun, and he'd have

JOHN TUNSTALL'S MURDER

been unlikely to use one to initiate a confrontation with men armed with rifles. Moreover, Morton's posse included Tom Hill, a notorious killer who'd been overheard saying that he'd be willing to kill John Tunstall, and Jesse Evans, once Tunstall's friend but now an enemy. Others in the posse were William M. Johnson, Ham Mills, Johnny Hurley, Frank Baker, and several Mexicans.

As the writer Emerson Hough later wrote about the incident, when the posse caught up with Tunstall they called for him to halt. He did. Tunstall asked if they would hurt him. Tom Hill said, "Hello, is that you?" and then pulled out his six-shooter and shot Tunstall. Another bullet was fired, and then a young Mexican boy named Pantilon bashed in Tunstall's skull with a rock. Tunstall's horse was also killed. The autopsy done on Tunstall showed two bullet wounds, a nonfatal one to his chest and a fatal one to his head.

Another account says that Jesse Evans first shot Tunstall in the chest, then Morton shot him in the head and bashed his skull with the butt of his rifle.

No doubt exists that the posse's mission was to kill Tunstall.

When Tunstall's men heard the commotion, they feared the worst; they scrambled up a nearby hill. From there, Billy the Kid and the other cowboys watched in horror and outrage. Billy the Kid swore vengeance on those who'd killed Tunstall. Billy was not alone. Those emotions and the cycle of violence and reprisals that followed escalated into the Lincoln County War.

I thought about Tunstall as my wife and I began the short hike down Tunstall Canyon to the murder site. I saw him on his horse, herding other horses, maybe chatting with the other cowboys—having no inkling that in an hour he would be dead.

I reflected that most people approach death that way.

Somber thoughts, in a somber forest. But then I don't really know what the vegetation was like in 1878. Perhaps, unlike today, trees were absent from the canyon, whether from logging or grazing or fire.

CHAPTER SEVENTEEN

James Dolan. Courtesy of the Palace of the Governors Photo Archives (NMHM/DCA), negative 000-742-1661.

Lawrence Murphy. Courtesy of the Palace of the Governors Photo Archives (NMHM/DCA), negative 000-742-0011.

If Tunstall's cowboys were intending to drive their stock down the canyon, they'd have had a hard time of it. Near the murder site, at the canyon's head, the slopes are gentle, with small meadows. But farther down the canyon narrows, becoming rough and rocky.

Perhaps Tunstall didn't plan to descend the canyon at all but rather intended to stay high in the mountains, over much easier terrain, until an easier descent could be found.

They might have been talking about the injustice of the court order, about what scoundrels the Murphy-Dolan-Riley crew were, about their own plans to camp in the river valley ahead, about what they'd do in Lincoln, the purchases they'd make, the business they'd attend to, the people they'd see.

All nullified by two gunshots at this place.

The sun was setting when my wife and I arrived at the murder site. From the village of Glencoe we'd driven the Coe Canyon Road (Forest Road 443) high into the mountains for about 4.5 miles to where Forest Road 443 and Forest Road 9019D joined (N 33 21 08 /

W 105 26 32). We parked nearby, then hiked to where Forest Road 9019D, a primitive road, descended to the head of Tunstall Canyon. The site is not far down, 0.3 miles and then about fifty yards west into the forest, marked by signs and a memorial. I mention this because my wife and I missed seeing the marker hiking down the canyon, and we hiked more than a mile beyond the spot before realizing we'd missed it. Hiking back uphill over a two-track road, we found the site. Not easy to miss, really, but we did.

At the site, the spindly second-growth pines cast long shadows over the scene. After photographing the site and getting a GPS location (N 33 21 50 / W 105 26 08), I sat for a moment. I chose not to imagine the brutal murder itself, reluctant to see young Tunstall lying on the ground, his head crushed. It was easier to imagine Billy's outrage, but even then I couldn't avoid imagining the Tunstall cowboys returning to the site to retrieve Tunstall's shattered body.

Nothing about the site suggests its significance. Rather, it's just a small, unremarkable clearing in an unremarkable patch of second-growth forest, many of the scraggly pines dead or dying,

The Tunstall murder site. Photo by Robert Julyan.

CHAPTER SEVENTEEN

the junipers and undergrowth also unkempt. There is no grassy meadow, no stream or spring; it's not a place one would come to for a picnic. Not a place where a young man would choose to die, but then people rarely get to choose their place of death. I took my photos and did not linger.

Tunstall's cowboys had witnessed a brutal, cold-blooded murder. In the best of times the deed would have cried out for frontier eye-for-an-eye vengeance—but this crime had been committed by a sheriff's posse.

Billy and the other Tunstall partisans soon formed a gang bent on administering their own justice; they called themselves the Regulators, and they quickly accomplished their goal of killing the men in the posse who had killed Tunstall. But the violence didn't stop there; retribution begat retribution until the region was riven by opposing outlaw gangs.

The Lincoln County War ended in a tragic, fiery death in Lincoln on July 19, 1878, at the end of a five-day siege reminiscent of World War I stalemates. Alexander McSween's home, which also served as the base for the Regulator faction, was burned. McSween was shot trying to escape. His wife survived the violence and went on to become a legendary figure in southern New Mexico ranching as Susan McSween Barber, "the Cattle Queen of New Mexico." The war had finally burned itself out.

Well, almost. There were several more deaths as Sheriff Pat Garrett and his men tracked down and killed former Regulators Billy the Kid, Charlie Bowdre, and Tom O'Folliard. I thought again of Tunstall as my wife and I hiked back to our car. I looked up at the hill from which Billy and the others had witnessed the murder. I could easily sympathize with their emotions. I'd have felt the same way. Billy once said of Tunstall, "He was the only man that treated me like I was free-born and white."

By all accounts, Tunstall was a decent man, the only one to attempt a nonviolent resolution of the feud, and with tragic irony the first to die. The Lincoln County War epitomizes what

Mahatma Gandhi said about vengeance: "An eye for an eye only ends up making the whole world blind."

To Learn More

Visit the peaceful little town of Lincoln, which serves as a living museum of this violent era.

Read *The Life and Death of John Henry Tunstall*, by Frederick W. Nolan (Santa Fe, NM: Sunstone Press, 2009).

Read *The Lincoln County War: A Documentary History*, by Frederick W. Nolan (Norman: University of Oklahoma Press, 1992).

Read some of the countless other books and browse the websites pertaining to the Lincoln County War. This aspect of New Mexico history remains controversial, and, as with the story of Oliver M. Lee (see chapter 18), I am too ill informed—and perhaps too cowardly—to dive in with an opinion of my own.

CHAPTER EIGHTEEN

Dog Canyon

IN THE OFTEN-TOLD folklore, genuine and apocryphal, about New Mexico's late nineteenth-century Apaches, a repeated theme is their mourning the loss to white invaders of their Dog Canyon in the Sacramento Mountains. Many Apaches were born there; they drank the clear water of its springs, ground grains in stone mortars, harvested and roasted mescal, and sought refuge beneath its towering limestone cliffs. And, ultimately, many died there, defending it.

But the events surrounding Apache–US Army conflicts in the canyon certainly are only those that have been recorded and have captured our imagination. Dog Canyon's human history begins long before the Apaches arrived in the region, with peoples whose identities and names have been forgotten.

Archaeological surveys indicate that humans began living in the canyon at least six thousand years ago, and likely much earlier, for no peoples living in the area would have ignored its obvious advantages. Most important was water. The Sacramento Mountains' western escarpment north and south of the modern town of Alamogordo is conspicuously dry, but natural springs at Dog

CHAPTER EIGHTEEN

Canyon's mouth and also along its course are relatively reliable sources of the precious liquid.

These water sources also would have nourished the plants and animals so important to the Native peoples. From willows they'd have made baskets and analgesic concoctions; from yuccas they'd have woven cordage and eaten the flowers and roots; creosote bush had numerous medicinal uses; the agave, or mescal, was an important food (the name Mescalero is derived from the Apaches' practice of roasting the plants' roots); they'd have crushed mesquite beans for food and used the gum as an antiseptic; and they'd have used numerous other plants for medicines or food: Mormon tea, four-wing saltbush, wolfberry, rabbitbrush, and others. They'd have hunted deer, javelinas, desert bighorn sheep, rabbits, and other desert animals. When I visited the springs at the height of a three-year drought, I found the air alive with birds and insects of numerous species. Water was flowing.

All this was critical to nomadic hunter-gatherers as the canyon provided a natural route between the hot, arid plains of the Tularosa Valley and the cool mountain meadows above. It was the route the Apaches used to travel from the valley to the Sacramento and Guadalupe Mountains. Even as late as the 1960s, Fairchild Ranch cowboys were driving stock up the canyon to high mountain pastures.

Curiously, only one Apache band is known to have lived in the canyon for any length of time—the Tsebekinéndé (known to Mexicans and Americans as Agua Nueva Mescaleros) in the 1850s and 1860s. During this period, they were led by an Apache whom non-Indians called Mateo, along with a man Spanish speakers called Verancia. Local non-Apaches called this group "troublesome."

But several other Apache bands, including the Ch'laandé/Tslahahéndé (Antelope Band People), who lived west of the Pecos in the mountains of central and southern New Mexico, and the Nit'ahéndé/Niit'ahéndé (People Who Live Against the Mountains; or, Earth Crevice / Deer People), who lived in the Sacramento and Guadalupe Mountains, also considered Dog Canyon within their territory.

Dog Canyon. Photo by Robert Julyan.

And the Mescaleros have had close ties with the Chiricahua Apaches from southwestern New Mexico and eastern Arizona; the famous Chiricahua leaders Geronimo and Nana both visited Dog Canyon. It was renowned throughout the larger Apache community.

So it was inevitable that when Apaches and white settlers clashed in the 1800s, Dog Canyon would be the scene of several battles. Each time I've hiked into Dog Canyon I've experienced a curious foreboding. I imagine myself a US soldier about to enter a place from which I might not return. Now on a hot July morning I am back, drawn by the canyon's dramatic human history but even more by its spectacular natural history.

My hike begins with 0.6 miles of steep switchbacks from the visitors' center to the relatively level shelf along the canyon's south side. A sign at the visitors' center warns me to beware of rattlesnakes.

CHAPTER EIGHTEEN

Yuccas along the trail into Dog Canyon. Photo by Robert Julyan.

It's a warning I take seriously, as once on an earlier occasion, when I'd spent a hot night sleeping on top of a picnic table in a campground, a rattlesnake moseyed by my site. While I couldn't imagine the snake returning, slithering up onto the table, and gratuitously biting me, I nonetheless slept uneasily that night. Two species, the western diamondback and the black-tailed, live in the canyon; of the two, the black-tailed is supposed to be the less aggressive, but I'd not want to put it to the test.

The hiking becomes easier as I reach the shelf and enter the canyon proper. From the visitors' center to the back of the canyon is three miles, and the park has placed distance markers every quarter mile. The trail is well traveled and easy to follow.

The beginning of the relatively easy hiking is where I begin asking: Was it here the troops were ambushed? Was it from behind these boulders that Apaches fired rifles and arrows at the soldiers?

Water at the mouth of Dog Canyon. Photo by Robert Julyan.

Historians have recorded at least five battles, or at least skirmishes, in the canyon. The first occurred in 1849 when Brevet Major Enoch Steen of the First Dragoons and thirty men of Company H, Second Dragoons, pursued Apaches who had killed several Mexicans forty miles south of Santa Fe. They overtook the Apaches near Dog Canyon and in the ensuing battle three troopers and five Indians were killed.

Then in 1853 a Mescalero band raided a California emigrant train near Van Horne, Texas, driving off 150 head of stock. The emigrants pursued the raiders and recovered the stock but were ambushed following the trail into Dog Canyon.

Perhaps the most memorable conflict occurred on February 8, 1859, when Lieutenant Henry Martyn Lazelle and thirty-two soldiers were ordered by commanders at Fort Bliss to pursue Apaches who allegedly had stolen cattle and three mules from San Elizaro, Texas. The Apaches had a three-day head start. Nonetheless, at

CHAPTER EIGHTEEN

noon of the seventh day, the troops, after a march of 165 miles, desperately thirsty, found themselves at the mouth of Dog Canyon.

Lazelle's report said that they overtook the Indians about 2.5 miles into the canyon. They counted about thirty warriors—"all stripped, painted, and armed." The Indians raised a white flag and wanted to parley. Lazelle demanded the return of the stolen animals, but the Apaches denied having them.

Lazelle then planned a predawn attack, but in the meantime the Indians received reinforcements, and they ambushed the soldiers as they moved up the canyon. Now outnumbered, Lazelle's men tried to withdraw, but the Indians blocked their retreat until eventually they escaped.

During the 1860s US Army soldiers pursuing Apaches found a stray dog in an abandoned camp. From that incident the canyon took its present name, only the latest of dozens it has had over the millennia.

Indian raiding in general intensified during the Civil War, when army troops were withdrawn to fight in the East. In response, in March 1863 Captain William McCleave and two companies of California troops were dispatched to quell the raiding. In Dog Canyon, likely near the head, they surprised a rancheria (encampment) of approximately five hundred Mescaleros—men, women, and children—and routed them. The Mescaleros fled to Fort Stanton, where they appealed to Colonel Kit Carson for peace. The Mescaleros' leader, Gian-na-tah, is reported to have made the following speech: "You are stronger than we, we have fought you as long as we had powder and rifles, but your weapons are better than ours. Give us such weapons and turn us loose and we will fight you again. But we're worn out, you have taken over and now you have our Dog Canyon. Do with us as you will, but remember, we are men and warriors."

That did not end the conflicts, however. In 1880 a detachment of the Ninth Cavalry pursued Apaches into Dog Canyon and made the disastrous mistake of attempting to follow them over the so-called Eyebrow Trail. Located at the back of the canyon, it leads from the

The Apache leader Nana. Courtesy of the Palace of the Governors Photo Archives, 016321.

canyon to the high meadows and forest. It's a steep, narrow path across a cliff face with vertical cliffs above and below. The troops had made it about halfway across when the Indians hurled boulders upon them, killing several soldiers and forcing them to retreat.

Apaches have their own memories of this incident. When a band of Warm Springs Apaches was fleeing the Mescalero Reservation, they were confronted by army troops being led by Apache scouts. They had to get to Tularosa Basin. "Where will we cross the plain?" one asked. "At Dog Canyon," another answered.

James Kaywaykla, a young boy with the band, later recounted the discussion in the book *In the Days of Victorio: Recollections of a Warm Springs Apache*, recorded by Eve Ball. Kaywaykla recalled the advice of Suldeen, another Apache warrior in the group:

> It is a good place to ambush the Blue Coats. . . . I know the place well. There is a narrow, winding trail leading into it. The

CHAPTER EIGHTEEN

entrance is not very wide, and between it and the narrow gap a short distance back is a spring. Beyond it, the walls are so close together that only one horse at a time can pass, and to do so he must scramble up a waist-high ledge. For an enemy coming in from the basin it is a death trap. The Mescaleros, and Nana too, have sent two or three on to the floor to lure cavalry into ambush. Once through the narrow opening with its perpendicular walls they can be killed with rocks from above.

The end came in dramatic fashion in 1881 when the Chiricahua chief Nana—Apache names Kas-tziden (Broken Foot) or Haskenaditla (Angry/Agitated)—left his sanctuary in Mexico and came to Dog Canyon. More than eighty years old, half-blind, and crippled with arthritis, he led approximately thirty warriors on the final epic chapter of the Apache Wars. The saga began when Nana and his band ambushed a pack train led by Lieutenant John F. Guilfoyle in nearby Alamo Canyon, killing a packer named Burgess and another man. Nana then fled to Dog Canyon, with Guilfoyle in pursuit. Despite a skirmish at nearby White Sands in which the Indians lost several animals and all their provisions, Nana escaped and embarked upon an epic reign of terror in the Southwest—raiding and eluding as many as a thousand army troops at a time, as well as several hundred militia members and Indian scouts. The raiding ended only when Nana slipped back over the Mexican border. Rarely have so few eluded so many.

Thus ended the battles in and around Dog Canyon.

But as compelling as Dog Canyon's human history is, the canyon itself is even more fascinating.

Like so many ranges in New Mexico's Basin and Range Province (physiographic region), the Sacramento Mountains were formed when a large block of the earth's crust subsided (the Tularosa Valley) and adjacent blocks rose (the San Andres Mountains on the west and the Sacramento Mountains on the east). Across desert flats of gypsum and mesquite, the mountains' steep escarpments face each other, exposing the same rock strata. In the Sacramentos, the steep western slopes rise to a crest, where they meet gently inclined slopes on the east.

Like other canyons on the range's rugged west face, Dog Canyon has been incised into eight thousand feet of mostly Paleozoic sedimentary rock, and as you hike you can find crinoid fossils in the pale limestone rocks. Although they look like plants, crinoids actually were animals.

Interspersed with the sedimentary limestone and sandstone are volcanic deposits. Along the trail I found outcrops of anomalous rock that looked like gray rocky road ice cream. The technical term for it is igneous porphyritic andesite.

This is the Chihuahuan Desert, and the plants here are typical of that harsh but seductive environment: sotol, agave, mesquite, century plant, creosote bush, and cacti. Especially cacti. I could spend an entire day happily fossicking around Dog Canyon looking for the canyon's numerous cacti. In a wet year, the canyon would be breathtaking with wildflowers.

And even now, in a year of drought, the riparian areas along the canyon's bottom crease are a vivid green, hosting birds and insects in great numbers and diversity. The Oliver M. Lee Memorial State Park at the canyon's mouth has a nature trail through the riparian area as well as an impressive garden of Chihuahuan Desert plants. Sitting in the cool shade of an evergreen oak, on a bench provided by the park, watching birds and dragonflies and butterflies, is a good alternative to hiking in the heat.

The Apache–US Army period of Dog Canyon's history lasted a mere forty years, less time than many readers of this account may have lived, but the canyon's natural history is timeless. Explore, enjoy, but beware of rattlesnakes.

Oliver M. Lee and "Frenchy" Rochas

Any discussion of Dog Canyon and its history would be incomplete without mentioning Oliver Milton Lee and Francois-Jean

CHAPTER EIGHTEEN

"Frenchy" Rochas. Frenchy moved to Dog Canyon from northern New Mexico in 1886 and settled at the mouth of Dog Canyon, where he tapped the perennial spring there to create a small agricultural enterprise based on gardening, vineyards, orchards, and ranching. Lee, originally from Texas, moved to Dog Canyon in 1893 and began ranching and farming. Together they built an irrigation system.

Frenchy's history in the canyon ended in 1894 when he was found shot in the chest in his cabin. A coroner's inquest concluded that he had shot himself—with his rifle. To many, this verdict was implausible; he was murdered, they said, and the likely suspect was Lee.

Lee also was suspected of being behind the murder of his bitter enemy Albert J. Fountain and Fountain's young son, who were killed while traveling through White Sands between Las Cruces and the Tularosa Valley. Their bodies have never been found, but there is no doubt that they were intercepted and murdered. Lee was an obvious suspect because of his rancorous relationship with Fountain, and he in fact stood trial at Hillsboro for the crime, but in the absence of conclusive evidence he was acquitted, which did nothing to quell rumors and suspicions that persist to this day. Lee remained a powerful and influential figure in New Mexico politics until his death in 1941.

The hike into Dog Canyon begins at Oliver M. Lee Memorial State Park, which has exhibits about both Frenchy and Lee. Lee's home and the remains of Frenchy's cabin and garden are prominent features of the park.

Numerous books have been written about Lee and Frenchy and their presence at Dog Canyon, and curious readers can delve into them to draw their own conclusions. But this book is about history off-road, and the Lee-Frenchy sites are readily accessible by car.

The Mescaleros

It would be tempting to say that the Mescalero Apaches are gone from Dog Canyon, but in fact they are not. In 1883, after years of conflict with whites and unsuccessful attempts to share reservations with other tribes, they were given their own reservation in the Sacramento Mountains. There they have skillfully managed their tribal lands' resources to create one of the nation's most successful reservations. It's less than thirty miles from the town of Mescalero to Dog Canyon—and best of all, the Mescaleros can now travel to the canyon in a vehicle rather than on foot, as the old-time Apaches would have done.

To Learn More

Visit the visitors' center at Oliver M. Lee Memorial State Park, which has numerous exhibits relating to the canyon as well as paintings of events that occurred there. Anyone hiking into Dog Canyon should stop there first.

Read *The Mountains of New Mexico*, by Robert Julyan (Albuquerque: University of New Mexico Press, 2006), which has much information about the entire Sacramento Mountain range and its subranges, including hiking information.

Read *In the Days of Victorio: Recollections of a Warm Springs Apache*, recollections by James Kaywaykla as recorded by Eve Ball (Tucson: University of Arizona Press, 1970).

Read *Apache Voices: Their Stories of Survival as Told to Eve Ball*, by Sherry Robinson (Albuquerque: University of New Mexico Press, 2010).

Read *Santana: War Chief of the Mescalero Apache*, by Almer N. Blazer (Taos, NM: Dog Soldier Press, 1999). Blazer spoke the Mescalero language fluently and was a personal and trusted acquaintance of the war chief.

CHAPTER NINETEEN

Waylaid

The Grave of William Grudging

WHEN THE APACHE danger in southwestern New Mexico ended with the surrender of Geronimo in 1886, one would have thought the region's endemic violence would have subsided, but it barely missed a beat. The new killers were the ranchers and homesteaders and settlers themselves. As Henry Woodrow, one of the first forest rangers of the Gila National Forest, recalled,

> During the [1890s], a new bunch of settlers came into the Gila area where most of the earlier settlers had been killed or run out by the Indians. Some of these new settlers were a different class of people. They brought in small bunches of cattle and settled on a small place and started farming on a small scale. By this time the Indians had quit killing people off, but these later settlers when they got tired of one another the best man with a gun killed his neighbor and got him out of the way.

This chapter is the story of several of those killings, and with

CHAPTER NINETEEN

The headstone of William Grudging's grave. Photo by Robert Julyan.

characteristic Gila irony they occurred along the sublimely beautiful and peaceful West Fork of the Gila River.

The hike along the West Fork begins at the parking area of Gila Cliff Dwellings National Monument (see page 166), at the end of the paved road. The hiking is easy, but like other hikes along the Gila River's branches it requires numerous river crossings; take old sneakers and a sturdy walking stick, and be aware that these crossings can be dangerous when the water is swift and high.

The trail meanders through a riparian area of willows, cottonwoods, Arizona sycamores, ponderosa pines, and junipers. After about half a mile, a spur trail leads across the river to a gravesite where a headstone reads, "William Grudging, waylayed [*sic*] and murdered by Tom Wood, October 8, 1883." (William Grudging's headstone says that he was murdered in 1883, but Woodrow states the incident occurred in 1893, which makes more sense.)

That is indeed what happened to William Grudging, but as so often happens, there's more to the story. In her book *Wilderness of the Gila*, Elizabeth McFarland allowed Woodrow to give a more complete account.

William Grudging and his brother, Tom, were newcomers to the Gila country. They built a cabin on the West Fork, not far from the gravesite, where it stood until destroyed by a forest fire.

The Grudgings may have had some cattle, but their main enterprise was jerking the meat of deer they killed and selling it in the booming mining camp of Mogollon. (The Jerky Mountains, Jerky Canyon, and Jerky Spring all owe their names to the Grudgings' enterprise.)

Problems arose when they expanded their operations to include not just deer meat but also beef, specifically from cattle belonging to other people, including those belonging to Thomas J. Wood. He'd been a peace officer in Iowa as a young man, fought in the Civil War, and prospected in California. (Prospecting in the Gila country, he'd found a dike of iron crossing a creek. Fortunately for the wilderness he found no other metals, but the creek still is called Iron Creek.)

CHAPTER NINETEEN

The cabin, since burned in a forest fire, where William and Tom Grudging lived near the West Fork of the Gila River. Photo by Robert Julyan.

Wood learned of the Grudgings' rustling, and the Grudgings knew that Wood knew. Afraid that Wood would give them away, they determined to ambush and kill him and his son, Tom Jr. They knew that the two Woods sometimes made trips to Pinos Altos and Silver City, and they knew their route, which passed by the Grudgings' cabin.

One day they watched as two men, whom they believed to be Tom Wood and Tom Jr., passed their cabin, and they awaited their return. They were unaware that, instead of going himself, Tom had sent a Mexican employee to accompany his son. The Grudgings watched as the two men returned, and knowing where they likely were going to camp that night, in a canyon just west of the Zig-Zag Trail, they followed them. There, in the darkness, the Grudgings shot and killed both of them. They thought they'd eliminated both father and son.

Tom Wood vowed revenge.

He concealed himself in a willow thicket near the Grudgings' cabin, and as the two Grudgings rode home on a road along a rail fence Wood opened fire, killing William. Thus was William Grudging "waylayed and murdered."

Tom Grudging, however, escaped. He fled the Gila country and went to Louisiana. Wood knew about this, but he had difficulty finding him there until an informant told Wood that he knew Tom Grudging and said that he would cross a certain Louisiana river at daybreak in a canoe.

Tom Grudging was missing a front tooth and had a habit of spitting through the gap. Wood knew he had his man when a fellow appeared who, upon reaching the canoe, spat in just such a manner. As Grudging climbed into the canoe, Wood stepped forward. "Hello, Tom," he said. Grudging, recognizing Wood, threw up his hands. Wood shot him.

Wood returned to the Gila country, where for two years he lived as an outlaw in the mountains. Finally he surrendered and stood trial in Silver City. In the parlance of the times, he "come clear," meaning that, although he had admitted to the killings, they were ruled justified.

Wood lived in Grant County for many years until his death. Henry Woodrow said that Wood had once showed him his gun, with fourteen notches, one for each man he'd killed. "He said many times that he wanted to get fifteen but never got to do this."

Next to William Grudging's grave is another, belonging to James Huffman, also a casualty of violence among early settlers. As Woodrow explained, Huffman and a rancher named Jordan Rodgers ran cattle in the area, their herds mingling. Huffman was a bully and had threatened Rodgers's life. Intimidated, Rodgers was afraid to go and work his cattle.

One day Rodgers was riding up the West Fork with a man called Buck Powell (he had changed his name from Murray when he arrived in the Gila country to elude law officers from Texas). Near a cabin at the mouth of EE Canyon they encountered Huffman, and an altercation ensued; Powell shot Huffman once, and Rodgers, not certain that Huffman was dead, fired several more shots into him.

CHAPTER NINETEEN

The West Fork of the Gila River. Photo by Robert Julyan.

Rodgers stood trial and, to repeat the phrase, "come clear." (Powell later was killed in a row in the mining town of Fairview, now called Winston.)

To reach Grudging's and Huffman's graves, hike slightly more than half a mile north from the trailhead to N 33 14 05 / W 108 16 17.8, to where a trail heads southwest to cross the river; take this trail about a third of a mile to the gravesite (N 33 14 05.75 / W 108 15 34.7). The Grudgings' cabin was immediately south of the gravesite, but it burned down in a forest fire.

Gila Cliff Dwellings

Another place of beauty and tragedy in the Gila Wilderness is Gila Cliff Dwellings National Monument. One of the Southwest's premiere archaeological sites, Gila Cliff Dwellings stands as a silent reminder that an advanced Indian civilization once thrived in southwestern New Mexico seven hundred years ago.

The site was inhabited by members of the Mogollon culture, widespread throughout southern New Mexico, who included the Mimbres culture along the Mimbres River. The Mogollon people were closely related culturally to the Ancestral Puebloan culture of Chaco Canyon to the north.

In AD 1275 the Mogollon people began constructing houses, storage units, and other structures in five linked caves overlooking Cliff Dweller Creek, using blocks of local volcanic conglomerate held in place with hand-pressed mortar; the handprints of the builders are still visible, as are cobs of the corn they ate. Dendrochronology (tree-ring dating) allows us to date the construction with great precision.

With great effort they quarried the blocks, hauled water to mix mortar, and transported timbers to create their village in this obscure, remote location. Then, after only twenty-five years, they left, part of the general exodus of Mogollon peoples from this region around this time. (The San Juan Plateau and much of northern Arizona were also abandoned about this time or earlier.) We don't know for sure where they went, and more intriguingly, we don't know why.

Other, much smaller cliff dwellings exist in the area. If you hike the West Fork Trail, you will come to Three-Mile Ruin. *Please* do not climb into the ruin; there's nothing inside to see, and it's extremely fragile.

To Learn More

Read Elizabeth McFarland, *Wilderness of the Gila* (Albuquerque: University of New Mexico Publications Office, 1974).

Read *The Gila Wilderness: A Hiking Guide*, by John A. Murray (Albuquerque: University of New Mexico Press, 1988). This book includes information about the Mogollon culture, whose people built the Gila cliff dwellings.

CHAPTER TWENTY

Cooney

Miners and Apaches in the Gila Country

THE GREAT IRONY of the Gila Wilderness is that a place of such sublime beauty and profound peace should have such a violent, tragic history.

I thought of that one January as I drove my Subaru Forester up US 180 from Silver City through the fertile valley of the San Francisco River. The scenery was similarly pleasant when I turned east from Alma to follow a good dirt road along the floodplain of Mineral Creek. Green pastures and open forests of pines, junipers, cottonwoods, and Arizona sycamores flanked the road, while nearby Mineral Creek burbled its winter song.

Five pretty miles ahead was the boulder-sepulcher of James C. Cooney and still farther the mining camp that bore his name. He was among the ironic Gila tragedies.

Born in Canada, Cooney was described as a "red-haired Irishman"; he moved to the United States and joined the army. In 1870 he was assigned to the Eighth Cavalry at Fort Bayard, near Silver City, becoming the fort's quartermaster. He earned the esteem of his fellow soldiers when he led a party that rescued Lieutenant

CHAPTER TWENTY

The site of the Cooney mining camp. Photo by Robert Julyan.

George M. Wheeler, who was surrounded by two hundred Apaches on a mountain in Arizona. Cooney's horse was shot, he took three arrows through his clothing, and three other men were also wounded. Seventeen Apaches were killed.

For his leadership, he was offered a commission, but he declined it. He had other priorities. While on patrol with the army in the Mineral Creek area, he had found what appeared to be a ledge of rich silver ore. After leaving the army in 1876, he and five other miners returned the following spring to file claims. But the Apache danger prevented them from actually working their claims until 1878. Cooney's mine was called the Silver Bar, but it was better known as the Cooney Mine. He and his associates worked their claims in earnest until April 29, 1880.

That would have been a fine spring day, clear, with cold water in the creek, the elms and sycamores bearing new leaves, wildflowers in the meadows, and towering canyon walls beneath the

The rock tomb of James Cooney and family members. Photo by Robert Julyan.

preternatural blue sky of southwestern New Mexico. A good day to be a relatively young man—Cooney was forty—working rich silver claims with friends.

Or a good day to be a young Apache warrior with a raiding party led by the renowned Victorio, that has just come across a group of white men who appeared to be easy victims.

The Apaches struck. Two miners were killed outright. Two others, one badly wounded, fled to warn settlers at nearby Alma. At the Roberts Ranch, settlers and miners used a crude stockade to repel the Indian attack. The following morning two miners, Cooney and William Chick, seeing no sign of the Indians, attempted to return to the mine to check on the men left there, but they were halted by an ambush.

That afternoon, the two tried again. They were killed.

Later, other rescuers found their scalped and "horribly mutilated" bodies. Nearby was a large boulder. The miners tunneled

CHAPTER TWENTY

into it and put "the fragments" of the miners' bodies inside, then sealed it with a door of colored stones and cement.

As I stood near Cooney's tomb, unmistakable beside the road (N 33 24 49 / W 108 50 13), I reflected on what must have been a horrific scene. Naked pieces of bodies, blood, the horror not lessened by knowing that two more bodies awaited in the Cooney mining camp. Yet my mind heard no echoes of that violence in the peaceful forested valley.

The road soon ended at a corral (N 33 25 06 / W 108 49 45), and I began following a trail up Cooney Canyon to the mining camp. I entered the narrow canyon, often less than fifty feet across, lined with the frozen waters of Mineral Creek. Slippery hiking. The creek is flanked by vertical tawny cliffs of volcanic andesite eroded into pillars, spires, arches, and caves: a place of shadows and sudden sunlight. Hiking here, I found it much easier to imagine an ambush.

Now the only the danger is from flash floods, not Apaches. Debris high on the canyon walls testify to violent floodwaters. A hiker in the canyon would be in a death trap. Now, in midwinter, the only hazard was slipping on the ice on the frozen stream.

Eventually the canyon became a little wider, about one hundred yards across; the sun shone, warm even in January, and the creek burbled. Soon I began finding signs of human activity: collapsed sheds, discarded mining equipment, slabs of rusted iron and tin, and, at what my GPS said was the actual site of Cooney's camp (N 33 25 20.5 / W 108 48 19), a small leveled area and stone walls. Supposedly, a flash flood in 1911 had swept away most of the camp. I saw no signs of mining—no mine dumps, adits, or pits—but the mines had not been by the stream but rather in the nearby hills.

Again, in the bright January sunlight, among the awakening trees and stream, imagining bodies strewn about was difficult—yet they were never far from my consciousness.

The Cooney story didn't end with Cooney's death. His brother, Michael, a Civil War veteran, upon hearing what happened to his brother, came to New Mexico. He took over his brother's mine, and apparently at least two of Michael's children were born here, because two of them are also interred in the boulder, along with their uncle.

At one time, the camp had six hundred residents and boasted three stamp mills—the ruins of one are less than a mile downstream (N 33 25 14 / W 108 49 57)—a school, a church, two hotels, and a post office. But declining metal prices and the 1911 flood killed the camp far more effectively than Victorio. Like James Cooney, Victorio's triumph was short-lived. Less than six months after Cooney's death, Victorio was killed by Mexican troops in Mexico at the Tres Castillos massacre.

As for Mike Cooney, he was destroyed by the same lust for treasure that had led his brother to his death. Mike spent the last part of his life prospecting, roaming the vast mountain wilderness of southwestern New Mexico (usually alone), and staying out longer and longer, searching for a rich vein such as his brother had found. In 1914, when Cooney was in his seventies, he left Socorro for yet another trip; he never returned. "It was a month or two before his body was found beside a large juniper tree where a side canyon goes into Sycamore Canyon," recalled Henry Woodrow, an early Gila Wilderness ranger. "The tree was marked with a blaze, and Cooney's body was packed out and buried at Socorro. Several years later I named that canyon for him, and it is still known as Cooney Canyon, but the gold mine has never been found." Southwestern New Mexico has four Cooney Canyons, one in the Black Range, one in the Gila Wilderness, one near Mount Withington, and the one I hiked. The man who named the canyon for Cooney said that it connected with Sycamore Canyon, but I haven't been able to find the link between the two canyons.

The story of the Cooney massacre continues. In 1980 the activist environmental organization Earth First! erected a monument, later destroyed by locals, beside Cooney's tomb dedicated to Victorio for his successful raid on Cooney and the killing of Cooney and his fellow miners. It read, in part, "This monument celebrates the 100th anniversary of the great Apache chief Victorio's raid on the Cooney

CHAPTER TWENTY

mining camp near Mogollon, New Mexico on April 12, 1880 [*sic*]. Victorio strove to protect these mountains from mining and other destructive activities of the white race. The present Gila Wilderness is partly a fruit of his efforts."

That's a bit of a stretch. After all, the Apaches had but six more desperate years before Geronimo's surrender in 1886, and with the Apaches gone the miners returned. What really saved the Gila country was a relative lack of valuable ores (except copper).

But without doubt the Apache presence in the region during the crucial exploratory phase limited and delayed development. For the same reason, much of southeastern New Mexico was not settled until the Comanches were gone.

The Cooney mining camp prospered until the metal market collapsed and the 1911 flood swept away most of the town, but the hike to its site is both beautiful and interesting—the Gila country as it should be, not as it too often has been.

Driving back to US 380, I stopped again at Cooney's bouldersepulcher. This time I noticed the tiny cemetery surrounding it, about five graves, at least two for children. "Gone but not forgotten," read one headstone, except that they *were* forgotten. What had been their stories? Many of the names were gone, others barely legible. How had *they* died?

I continued driving through Mineral Creek Valley. Peaceful, tranquil, beautiful, the Arizona sycamores almost ornamental. But then I glanced toward the little creek, still burbling cheerfully, then the rest of the floodplain: stumps, trunks, broken limbs, boulders, sand, and gravel. Not too long ago a flash flood—crashing, shrieking, foaming, angry brown water—had scoured the valley. Then all had become calm and peaceful again.

I doubt I will ever understand the Gila country.

Another Miner's Good Fortune Cut Short

The sad fate of James C. Cooney, a relatively young man who enjoyed his great discovery all too briefly, is paralleled by another

Apache incident that occurred less than a hundred miles away. In 1878, as Cooney and his miners were trying to validate their silver claims, George Daly bought a silver claim at Lake Valley, in the Black Range's eastern foothills. While working his claim, Daly discovered an ore body that was the richest anyone in the area had seen. Ore could be removed with saws. It was called the Bridal Chamber, and it yielded 2.5 million ounces of silver.

On the day he discovered the Bridal Chamber, Daly was killed by Apaches, leaving the riches he discovered to be mined by others.

One Final Note

An important incident related to the Apache conflict that I was forced to omit from this book because of public access issues is the infamous McComas massacre. In the spring of 1883 Silver City judge Hamilton McComas, his wife, Juniata, and their six-year-old son, Charlie, set out in a wagon on an urgent legal errand in Lordsburg. The trip was ill advised, as Apaches were known to be raiding, and when seventeen miles from Silver City the party stopped for the night at Mountain Home Inn, they again were urged not to continue. Judge McComas, however, may have thought the raiding was farther west.

The next morning they continued. At the mouth of Thompson Canyon on the west side of the Burro Mountains, they stopped for a picnic at a large walnut tree. Suddenly, Apaches led by Chato appeared. The judge and his wife were killed—he was shot, she brained with a rock—and their bodies mutilated. Little Charlie was kidnapped.

The region, indeed the nation, was outraged. Heretofore, most victims of Apache raids, uncounted hundreds of them, had been nobodies—cowboys, sheepherders, prospectors, freighters—people that few knew. But Judge McComas and his family were different; newspapers across the country told the story of their murders. The nation became obsessed with the fate of Charlie. But despite

CHAPTER TWENTY

a region-wide search that lasted years, even decades, Charlie was never found. Apaches are consistent in saying that he was killed but differ as to whether this occurred soon after his capture or later by an angry Apache—bashing his head against a rock in both versions.

A line had been crossed. The Apache menace had to end.

So, without intending to, Chato had sealed his fate and that of free Apaches in the Southwest.

General George Crook requested and received hot-pursuit permission to enter Mexico. Relentlessly he and his men pursued the raiding Apaches, led by Apache guides often of the same band as the Apaches they were pursuing. With no refuge anywhere, Apache resistance was futile. In September 1886 Geronimo surrendered in Skeleton Canyon in the Peloncillo Mountains, just over the border from New Mexico in Arizona. The Apache Wars were over.

Chato was twenty-three when his party killed the McComas family. Later, he became an army scout, but after that he was taken prisoner, sent to Washington, DC, and then imprisoned at Fort Madison in Saint Augustine, Florida, along with five hundred other Apaches. He died in 1934.

While you can't visit the McComas massacre site, you can see it on Google Earth at N 32 33 38 / W 108 33 52.

To Learn More

Read *Ghost Towns and Mining Camps of New Mexico*, by James E. and Barbara H. Sherman (Norman: University of Oklahoma Press, 1975).

Read *Haunted Highways: The Ghost Towns of New Mexico*, by Ralph Looney (Albuquerque: University of New Mexico Press, 1979).

Read *Black Range Tales*, by James A. McKenna (Silver City, NM: High-Lonesome Books, 2002). First published in 1936, *Black Range Tales* has become a southwestern classic, giving first-person accounts of prospecting, Indian fights, exploration, boomtown life, and the characters of southwestern New Mexico. As one reviewer put it, "The result is alternately humorous, poignant, amazing or insightful; a singular look at the times. And most of all these tales are true, for by golly, James A. McKenna was there." There is much information about Victorio.

CHAPTER TWENTY-ONE

The Boneyard
Cookes Canyon

FOR PERHAPS THE first time in their multi-thousand-year history, Cookes Spring and Cookes Canyon aren't really important. People no longer travel by horses or foot, and water is just a short drive away by automobile at the Mimbres River or, even better, at the town of Deming, clean and treated. There's no reason to seek out a spring in the southern foothills of the Cookes Range or to make the journey shorter by taking a dangerous pass through the mountains. The Apaches who once lived and raided here are gone by more than a century, so there's no reason to maintain a military fort from which to launch campaigns. The adobe fort was left to disintegrate in the weather; now it sits in the middle of nowhere, difficult even to find.

Nonetheless, I'm here for the second time in two weeks, driving the same rough rocky road I drove a week ago when the road tore the splash guard from beneath my car's engine, ending that attempt to reach my destination. This time I drive much slower, but the five miles to Cookes Spring and Fort Cummings from NM 26 north are still an ordeal. Miles of creosote bush and desert scrub, nothing

CHAPTER TWENTY-ONE

green to indicate water. When I finally reach Fort Cummings in the flats at the canyon's mouth I am relieved, but that doesn't compare to what travelers would have felt who arrived by foot, horse, wagon, or stagecoach a hundred years ago. For them, the nearest reliable water to the east was at Mesilla, more than fifty miles away; the nearest to the west the Mimbres River, about twenty-five.

I'm here because of the canyon and its often-tragic history, but in fact everything that happened here stems from the spring. It has attracted humans for at least ten thousand years. And over those millennia, tens of thousands of people have made hundreds of thousands of treks through the canyon to and from the spring—and only a vanishingly small percentage experienced any violence. Yet the years between 1840 and 1886 stamped on the canyon a dark reputation that overshadows the positive benefits of the spring. During that forty-year period an unprecedented number of settlers, ranchers, and miners inundated the traditional lands of several Apache bands, who in turn invaded the traditional territories of still earlier inhabitants such as the Pimas and several other tribes, time out of mind. What defined this period of conflict between Native Americans and white settlers was the nature of the adversaries. The Apaches were a mostly nomadic Athabascan people, close relatives of the Navajos, who arrived in the Southwest probably around 1400. The Indians the Apaches encountered were primarily agricultural and thus obvious targets for raiding. When Spaniards arrived soon after, their villages also became raiding targets. Raiding was an ancient and honorable part of Apache culture, as it was for many Native groups around the world; the raiding season was part of the annual cycle.

But the Apaches were few in number and technologically primitive. To compensate, they became consummate guerrilla fighters, masters of ambush, stealthy, silent, and ruthless. It's hard to overstate the intensity of hatred that developed between the Apaches and other Indian tribes, then the Spanish, and eventually white American settlers.

Ultimately, it was unrelenting pressure from the American

The grave of John Chaffin, a forty-niner bound for the gold fields of California, who died here of natural causes in November 1849. Photo by Robert Julyan.

soldiers, many of them Civil War veterans, usually with Apache guides often from the same bands they were pursuing, that ended a very bloody period in American history.

But peace was far in the future when the canyon that lay ahead of me on this dirt road developed a reputation as the deadliest route in New Mexico. So frequent and deadly were the attacks here that it ceased being called Cookes Canyon and became Massacre Canyon. The peak nearby was called Massacre Peak.

No one is here on this bright sunny day in January. Before hiking, I look around Fort Cummings. It's a popular destination with four-wheelers, off-road vehicles, van campers, and jeepers, so roads snake through the area, not that there's much to see. The site is owned by the Hyatt family, whose ranch is nearby; they allow visitors who respect the site and follow the rules.

CHAPTER TWENTY-ONE

I walk through thickets of creosote bush to standing adobe walls, inexorably dissolving in the infrequent rains. Scenic and picturesque. Then to crumbling stone walls perched atop a small rise, likely the stage stop. And that's about it.

But it was not always so. The Bureau of Land Management's Las Cruces office has placed interpretive signs around the site with old photos showing a substantial installation. It was mostly a tent city but it also had a hotel, a trading post, livery stables, and various services for travelers.

Fort Cummings was not built to last. Like so many frontier outposts it was built quickly using the cheapest, most readily available material—adobe—for a specific purpose, guarding the spring and protecting travelers; and then, when the circumstances changed, it was abandoned. In fact, Fort Cummings was abandoned three times between its opening in 1863 and its final closure in 1886. It was not a place upon which to base a stable military career. One historian who visited Fort Cummings summarized what was likely the soldiers' general opinion of the place: "Life was hell inside the walls of Fort Cummings, but it was worse outside the walls."

As I walk around, I notice fragments of bottles, ceramics, metal, all the myriad debris people toss around at a military base.

With foreboding I walk to the cemetery, dreading to see the resting places of those who died horribly in the canyon, but I can spare my sensitivity: the bodies are no longer there. In 1892 they were transferred and reinterred in the National Cemetery at Fort Leavenworth, Kansas. Out of eighty reported burials, seventy-four were exhumed, including twenty-five unknowns. Unfortunately, Fort Leavenworth records show no reinterments from Fort Cummings. I hope the remains are in Kansas; if it were me, I certainly would not wish to be buried in the same alien no-man's-land where I'd been murdered.

In 1870 Maria Schrode stopped with her husband and eight children at Fort Cummings and visited the cemetery. "It is walled in with rough stones about five feet high, white washed [as was the front of the fort], with a folding gate. Some of the graves are walled with rock. I noticed six of them had been killed by the Apache Indians. There was only about 20 graves in all."

From Cemetery Ridge one views an uninhabited landscape of creosote bush, saltbush, and grass. During the Pleistocene Epoch more than 11,700 years ago, Paleo-Indians would have been the first humans drawn to the spring. The climate would have been cooler and wetter then, but they still would have noticed a reliable, permanent spring. The plains at that time would have resembled the Serengeti game plains in East Africa, with many of the same animals: lions, camels, elephant-like mastodons and mammoths, saber-toothed cats, giant sloths, horses, huge bison, and many more. The pass here through the southern extension of what is now the Cookes Range would have been a perfect place to ambush migrating animals.

Then the climate became warmer and drier. For reasons still debated, most of the Pleistocene megafauna went extinct. The Paleo-Indians were succeeded by hunter-gatherers who lived in what is termed the Archaic period. In these drier times, they would have valued the spring even more. And the canyon and the spring still would have been good hunting grounds. The Archaic hunter-gatherers lasted at least five thousand years, leaving almost no traces beyond a few atlatl dart points.

By two thousand years ago, the Archaic hunter-gatherers were becoming agriculturalists, eventually becoming the Ancestral Puebloans, here the Mimbres branch of the Mogollon culture. Then, around AD 1300, the Mogollon people vanished from the area. The next people to claim the region as their territory were the Apaches.

Because I do volunteer archaeological surveys for the Bureau of Land Management, by habit I'm always looking at the ground for artifacts. The ground here is littered with lithics, nonlocal chunks of flint or chert that had been chipped. Curiously, I see no potsherds, likely because they'd already been collected by soldiers and travelers but also because most of the Indians who had camped here in earlier eras were prepottery.

CHAPTER TWENTY-ONE

The first European to call attention to the spring and the pass was New Mexico governor-explorer Juan Bautista de Anza in 1780. He stopped here, looking for a route southwest into Chihuahua. He found a good route, but few used it.

Everything changed, however, in 1847 when Lieutenant Colonel Philip St. James Cooke led the Mormon Battalion by here en route to California. The Mormon Battalion was the only military unit in US history organized around religion. It had originally been mustered as an expeditionary force to seek out and seize a suitable seaport in California in anticipation of the establishment of the independent Mormon state of Deseret. The battalion had set out for the old mission of San Gabriel to rendezvous with Mormon spies when the Mexican War broke out. The Mormons concluded that they had more to gain, certainly in fostering better relations with Washington, by throwing in with General Stephen Watts Kearny in his campaign in the Southwest. Kearny appointed Cooke to lead the Mormon column.

For the next four months, marching over 1,100 miles, Cooke led the troops through some of the nation's most difficult terrain. The Mormons came to follow and respect him. In New Mexico the party acquired another guide, the adventurer and mountain man Jean Baptiste Charbonneau, the son of the Shoshone Indian Sacagawea, who had carried him as an infant across the Northwest with the Lewis and Clark Expedition.

The Mormon Battalion was a success, not only in the Mexican War but also in helping to validate US claims to the Southwest. And at least as important, they opened a southern wagon route to California. Cooke's orders were to march the Mormons to California and build a wagon road along the way.

I hope the place made an impression on him, because he made an impression on the place. Cookes Peak, Cookes Canyon, Cookes Spring, and the abandoned mining town of Cookes all were named for him.

His timing could not have been better. In 1848 gold was discovered at Sutter's Mill in California. A year later the Gold Rush began. Within seven years 150,000 people would travel by land for California, and many would go by the southern route.

Several entrepreneurs attempted to open stage lines, but the one that succeeded was the Butterfield Overland Mail. In 1857 John W. Butterfield and his associates were contracted to carry the US mail between Saint Louis and Memphis in the East and San Francisco in the West. They made their first run in 1858, and thereafter their crews made twice-weekly hell-bent-for-leather runs. It was dangerous work, but they usually made it.

For all its prominence in the iconography of the Old West, the Butterfield Overland Mail didn't really last long. It accrued significant debt. There was competition from the Pony Express, which was even less successful. And, conclusively, the Civil War siphoned off troops who otherwise would be protecting the mail routes. The federal troops protecting Cookes Spring and the nearby pass were withdrawn to the war in the East. The Overland Mail ended in March 1861. Less than ten years later the last spike would be driven in the transcontinental railroad. The days of long-distance travel using horsepower were ending. And while horse-drawn wagons were still operating, they were prey to the Apaches, who saw the pass as a natural ambush funnel.

It was time for me to visit the spring. It's in a grove of gray-green shrubs, not the bright green cottonwoods and other wetland plants I expected. It's enclosed within a round, head-high stone structure perhaps twenty feet in diameter, easily among the finest spring houses I've seen in New Mexico. It was built by the Atchison, Topeka and Santa Fe Railway in 1881; water flowed by gravity from here to the railroad at Florida Station, on NM 26 and Cookes Canyon Road, approximately 5.5 miles away. The roof was reconstructed in 1897.

When I visited, the spring was dry.

I was prepared for this possibility because I'd read a 2007 blog post that reported it dry, but I was still perplexed. How could this be? This spring had provided water for perhaps a hundred generations of people, determining the course of Western history—and now it was

CHAPTER TWENTY-ONE

The spring house at the mouth of Cookes Canyon. Photo by Robert Julyan.

dry? Admittedly, New Mexico had been in a severe drought, but I'd hoped for at least a little water from this particular source.

Finally I began hiking into the canyon, and I defy anyone to hike here without looking for possible ambush sites. None appeared immediately; in fact the terrain was surprisingly open. But then the canyon narrowed with beetling rocks overhead. I took photos and GPS readings, labeling them AMB 1 and AMB 2.

Before long, however, the canyon opened into a large, open valley. I'd have thought this would be terrible country for an ambush. But one mustn't underestimate the Apaches' ability to use small geographic features, such as minor arroyos, for concealment.

The maps I'd made showed graves, and I used my GPS to find the first one. There was no mistaking this initial site for a grave; I wonder if anyone knows who was buried here.

Farther up the basin was John Chaffin's grave. His death had nothing to do with Apaches. A "forty-niner," he'd taken ill on the pack train he was accompanying and died at Fort Cummings. The mystery of the Chaffin site is that the marker and historic marker mention only John Chaffin—but there are two graves.

Somewhat farther up was another grave, unmarked but also clearly a grave, in fact likely two graves laid out end to end. As I wandered into the canyon, I found dozens of suspicious rock outlines that could have been more graves—or not. One researcher estimated that fifteen graves are in the canyon.

The hiking was relatively straightforward, on a dirt road. I watched for obvious ambush sites, but for all I know their obviousness disqualified them from being *actual* ambush sites.

I don't know how many travelers died in Indian attacks in the canyon over the years. It was enough that the canyon lost the name Cookes Canyon and became Massacre Canyon. The estimated total deaths in Massacre Canyon varies widely. One source says around a hundred, including travelers, soldiers, and Indians. Bob Rockwell's estimate is four hundred; a Deming historian, Rockwell researched the canyon and wrote a novel about it, *In the Jaws of the Beast*. If he's correct, and others corroborate his estimate, that means an average of one death every forty feet. The canyon's deadliness is well documented. When stagecoach passengers complained about the number of corpses they could see along the route, an army detail was assigned to bring them in and bury them.

Indians also died in Massacre Canyon, although their graves are unmarked, their locations unknown. In the book *In the Days of Victorio: Recollections of a Warm Springs Apache*, Eve Ball recorded the memories of James Kaywaykla, who as a young boy had been with Victorio, Nana, and other well-known Apaches of the era. The Apache band, always fearful of discovery and pursuit, had left Ojo Caliente and the Black Range and moved southwest. They passed by Fort Cummings, where Nana showed himself as a decoy and drew troops away toward the Florida Mountains while the rest of his group entered Cookes Canyon. Suddenly Blanco, an Apache lookout on a small hill, raised his rifle, a sign they were being

CHAPTER TWENTY-ONE

pursued. They dashed for the hill, where Blanco said, "Dust behind you. Cavalry. Dismount and take cover."

Soon, a troop of "Buffalo Soldiers" (African Americans) led by a white officer appeared, apparently unaware of the Indians nearby. The Apaches opened fire. The soldiers fought back, then retreated, except for two who dashed into an arroyo. Blanco ran after them.

Others followed him. As Kaywaykla narrated, "We saw Blanco lying in the sand. Kaytennae and Suldeen [two Apache warriors] had gone on after the Negroes. As we bent over the body we heard more shots. . . . Under an overhanging bank Kaytennae and Suldeen scooped a hole in the sand. They placed Blanco's body in it, laid his rifle by him, and covered him with Mother's blanket. They piled rocks over the grave and collapsed dirt on it. Then we returned to the rest."

Another unknown grave, among many.

No, I'm not morbid, but terrible events occurred here that forever distinguish Cookes Canyon from other places in New Mexico. That they happened cannot be ignored.

The research I conducted for this book has required me to be in places where people died violently: the Tunstall murder, the Hermit's murder, the Cooney massacre, Dog Canyon, and the plane crash in TWA Canyon. Nonetheless, I was affected by this death site more than any other I've visited, perhaps because I had a better idea of the horror and the carnage that occurred here. Here were extremes of mutilation and torture.

In his novel *In the Jaws of the Beast*, Rockwell portrays two post–Civil War couples and their families, one from the North the other from the South, heading west to start over and heal wounds. They are assured by the military and everyone at Fort Cummings that no Apaches are in the area. The families are nevertheless attacked and massacred. Only one man survives with his freedom; his son is kidnapped and the rest are killed and mutilated.

The book, although fiction, contains elements of truth, as events such as this did happen. In one incident in the 1860s the frontiersman John Cremony was the first one on the scene after a party of Mexicans—eight men and their women and children—were tortured and killed in the canyon.

> One of the most cruel spectacles ever presented to my gaze occurred in Cookes Canyon. . . . A party of eight well-armed Mexicans, accompanied by their families . . . and having seven wagons . . . were on their way from Sonora to California, when they were set upon by nearly 200 savages in Cookes Canyon. The Mexicans defended themselves with undaunted courage, which forced the Apaches to resort to their accustomed cunning. . . . They then said that if the Mexicans surrendered their arms and gave them half the mules attached to the wagons they might prosecute their journey in peace with the remainder. This proposition was accepted . . . but each man was seized.

The narrative gets worse from there.

It was incidents such as this that forced the US Army in 1863, in the midst of the Civil War, to construct Fort Cummings.

Actually, the only battle between Apaches and US soldiers during the Civil War involved Confederate troops. In August 1861 a large party of Indian refugees from Tubac in southern Arizona were trying to reach the Rio Grande when they were set upon by Apaches in the canyon. The last wagon, carrying women and children, escaped to Pinos Altos and summoned the local Confederate garrison. Their commander, Thomas J. Mastin, shrewdly guessed that he wouldn't find the Apaches in the Cookes Range but rather farther south, in the Florida Mountains, where the Apaches had fled with the loot and stock from the Tubac refugees. At a pass there, Mastin waited with his troops. The Confederates routed the surprised Apaches and recovered most of the stock.

But the inevitable conclusion of this era in Western history was approaching. Fort Cummings was decommissioned for the last time in 1886. Transcontinental travel was now done by train, not by

CHAPTER TWENTY-ONE

stagecoach, and Cookes Canyon and Cookes Spring ceased to be important except for the history they'd witnessed.

To Learn More

View the photos in *New Mexico Then and Now*, by William Stone, with text by Jerold G. Widdison (Englewood, CO: Westcliffe Publishers, 2003). The contemporary photos by Stone were deliberately taken from the same perspective as the historic photos, and the contrast dramatically shows the changes that have occurred during the intervening years. The interesting text gives context to the historic sites.

Read *New Mexico: A New Guide to the Colorful State*, by Lance Chilton et al. (Albuquerque: University of New Mexico Press, 1984). This is perhaps my favorite New Mexico guide, covering all the state's regions and not just the Rio Grande corridor. It's long out of print, but copies still can be found and are worth looking for.

Read *On the Border with Crook: General George Crook, the American Indian Wars, and Life on the American Frontier*, by John Gregory Bourke, 3rd edition. (New York: Skyhorse Publishing, 2014). Bourke, longtime aide-de-camp to General Crook, provides a fascinating firsthand account from the American perspective of the American campaign against the Apaches in the Southwest.

Read *I Fought with Geronimo*, by Jason Betzinez and Wilbur Sturtevant Nye (Lincoln: Bison Books, University of Nebraska Press, 1987). Betzinez, Geronimo's cousin and a member of his band, recounts his years as a youth on the warpath, his capture and imprisonment in Florida, then his time at the Carlisle Indian Industrial School in Pennsylvania and his eventual assimilation into American society.

Read *In the Days of Victorio: Recollections of a Warm Springs Apache*, by Eve Ball and James Kaywaykla (Tucson: University of

Arizona Press, 1972). This is the memoir of James Kaywaykla, who was with the Apaches during one of their battles with the US Army in Cookes Canyon.

Read Bob Rockwell's novel about the canyon, *In the Jaws of the Beast* (n.p.: Desert Wind Books, 2012).

CHAPTER TWENTY-TWO

Persian Ibex in New Mexico

IT LIKELY WAS a bright, clear day in December 1970 when a New Mexico Department of Game and Fish helicopter landed in the Florida Mountains south of Deming. After touching down, the crew released fifteen ibex, which had been raised from birth in the Rio Grande Zoo in Albuquerque for quarantine reasons, into their new wilderness home. Soon thereafter, twenty-seven more were released. It was truly a historic moment, when the natural history of New Mexico—and the character of the Florida Mountains—changed forever.

Ibex (*Capra aegagrus*), also known commonly as Persian ibex, Persian wild goat, Iranian ibex, bezoar goat, and pasang, are found in the wild nowhere else in North America. In fact, to see other members of this species, you have to go to Iran, where they are native.

The idea of bringing this exotic species to New Mexico originated with Dr. Frank Hibben, an archaeologist and international big-game hunter who chaired the New Mexico Game and Fish Commission from 1961 to 1971. He had hunted large mammals in

CHAPTER TWENTY-TWO

habitats overseas similar to ones in New Mexico that had no big game species; he felt that ecological niches existed here that were unfilled. Two such niches were the desert grasslands of the White Sands Missile Range and the desert mountains of the Floridas. To fill the former, he proposed introducing the oryx, native to southern Africa's Kalahari Desert; they arrived in the Tularosa Basin in 1969. A year later, the ibex went to the Floridas.

Even after his death in 2002 Hibben has remained a controversial figure. As an archaeologist, he excavated such important sites as Sandia Man Cave in the Sandia Mountains and Pottery Mound along the Rio Puerco west of Los Lunas. He reported the discovery of the "Mystery Stone," inscribed with Paleo-Hebraic letters, on Hidden Mountain west of Los Lunas. The controversies that swirled around his career as an archaeologist are too complex for the purposes of this book, but hardly less controversial was his introducing the two exotic animal species into the New Mexico wilderness.

That's because, around the world, the introduction of nonnative species, no matter how well intentioned, has usually meant ecological disaster. Hares from Europe overran Australia. Mongooses from Southeast Asia have devastated Hawaii's bird life. Pythons are decimating fauna in the Florida Everglades. Throughout North America, starlings and English sparrows have become nuisances, competing with native birds. There are the Asian carp. Zebra mussels. The examples go on.

And here in New Mexico, plants such as tamarisk and Russian olive clog waterways, while knotweed and cheatgrass elbow aside native plants. What was Hibben thinking?

I'd been fascinated by the Florida Mountains ever since I first moved to New Mexico more than thirty years ago, not long after the ibex were introduced. The range's jagged profile reminds me of a mirage of a giant battleship floating in the desert. Like the Organ Mountains east of Las Cruces, they owe their appearance to volcanism associated with the spreading Rio Grande Rift. These volcanic rocks, overlaying Precambrian granite and sedimentary rocks,

Western face of the Florida Mountains, a perfect habitat for ibex, who easily traverse the cliffs. Photo by Robert Julyan.

typically weather into vertiginous cliffs and spires and towers, inspiring place names such as Castle Rock, Chimney Point, Lovers Leap Canyon, Needles Eye, Devils Arch, and Dragon Ridge: eminently photogenic, and conspicuously harsh and dry. Only during a wet spring, when yellow Mexican poppies blanket the mountains' foothills, do they live up to their Spanish name, which translates as "flowery."

I'd taken short hikes in the Floridas, mostly out of the Spring Canyon Picnic Area, part of Rockhound State Park in the Little Florida Mountains nearby to the northeast, but I felt I needed to experience the Floridas of the ibex. To do that I'd need to hike farther—and higher.

Fortunately, a neighbor of mine is an ibex hunter, and he told me where my chances of seeing one were good: Mahoney Park, a large *rincón* on the range's west side. So I drove my Subaru Forester over a rough dirt road to an abandoned stone cabin at the mountain's

CHAPTER TWENTY-TWO

base. I probably could have driven farther, but I wanted to experience the Floridas on foot.

Although roads such as the one I hiked exist in the range, along with abandoned mines and primitive cabins, the Floridas are managed as wilderness by the Bureau of Land Management, and rightly so. No one who has hiked here could consider the mountains as anything but wild. Certainly not the animals who live here: Gila monsters, javelinas, deer, mountain lions, coyotes, coatimundi, ringtails, golden eagles—and, of course, the ibex.

I stopped occasionally to "glass" the high peaks (as hunters refer to using binoculars or telescopes; no one looks for ibex in the Floridas without serious optics). A party of bow hunters I met said that the animals would be up high, in the cliffs, on ridgelines, their scimitar-shaped horns unmistakable against the sky.

I didn't have to worry about trees obscuring my view; except for low junipers, scrub oak, hackberry, and other low-lying desert species, the mountains are treeless. Vegetation is typical of the Chihuahuan Desert: creosote bush, yucca, agave, soaptree yucca, blue grama grass, and prickly pear and barrel cacti.

And the terrain is dry. Aside from a windmill-fed stock tank where I parked, I saw no evidence of springs, let alone streams. Later I searched my topographic maps and found only four springs in the entire range, all on the east side, but as I've learned from my years of hiking in New Mexico, labeled springs aren't necessarily reliable year-round.

Apaches knew how to find water here. When a group of Apaches in 1861 stole livestock from travelers they'd ambushed near Cookes Peak, they passed through the Floridas en route to sanctuary in Mexico. They were met by a contingent of the Confederate States Militia and lost eight warriors in the ensuing battle. In 1877 US Army troops fought a battle with Apaches led by Victorio, whose presence in the mountains is memorialized by the naming of Victorio Canyon. The encircled US troops finally broke free and escaped.

I passed several old mine dumps. Like other New Mexico ranges with similar geology, the Floridas had relatively little

PERSIAN IBEX IN NEW MEXICO

A big billy. Male Persian ibex in the Florida Mountains. Photo courtesy of the New Mexico Department of Game and Fish.

mineralization, although miners in the 1880s extracted $60,000 in lead, with smaller amounts of copper and silver.

The road I was following began climbing steeply and got much rougher. My neighbor had said that only someone who didn't value his vehicle would attempt driving it, but judging from the metal scrapes on boulders and broken car-body parts scattered around, many drivers had ignored that advice. The road was so rough that even hiking it was a chore.

I stopped at switchbacks to glass for ibex, but they eluded me.

I followed the road to a saddle, where I found another stone cabin, used by hunters. Then, following my neighbor's directions, I followed an old mine road until it ended, whereupon I struck out cross-country to the ridgetop. There I found a crude hunter's blind and a 360-degree view of the high mountains.

All around me were formidable, dark volcanic cliffs. I glassed

CHAPTER TWENTY-TWO

A herd of Persian ibex making their way across a cliff in the Florida Mountains. Photo courtesy of the New Mexico Department of Game and Fish.

them diligently but all too briefly because I still had to hike back to my car. No ibex. Just spectacular desert mountain scenery. To the southeast rose the hulking dome of Gym Peak, rising above the intervening ridge like a giant gray gumball.

But no ibex. My odds had been good. The New Mexico Department of Game and Fish's website claimed that the current population of ibex (as of January 2013) in the Floridas was 350 animals, to be culled by 125 animals when rifle-hunting season began a month later. From the original introduction of 42 ibex, the population has fluctuated from 300 to 800 animals. Clearly the ibex and the Floridas are compatible. In fact, as is so often true with introduced species, they have done far better in their new home than they had been doing in their native habitat. The ibex have no predators in the Floridas.

Except human hunters. Because, in the United States, ibex are found only here, and because hunters consider them to be spectacular trophies, and because bagging one is an extraordinary hunting challenge especially for bow hunters, hunters come from all over to stalk them. Ibex can use their suction-cup hooves to walk across cliffs, jump several times their own height, and spot movement half a mile away. In Deming there are several outfitters whose primary business is guiding ibex hunters.

My neighbor and a bow hunter I'd met that day—he'd seen dozens of ibex that day, but then he'd been in the mountains for twelve hours—are responsible hunters and keep the meat as well as the horns. But among New Mexico big-game hunters, opinions are mixed regarding the desirability of ibex steaks. As the bow hunter said, "They're not very good eating. After all, they're a goat." My neighbor said that seasonings definitely improve the taste.

So what's the verdict on Hibben's exotic introductions? Purists will say, "No exotics anywhere, anytime." The oryx long ago escaped from the missile range and now have expanded throughout southern New Mexico. They, like the ibex, are a much sought-after big-game animal for hunters. I'm withholding my judgment until I've seen one in the wild; they're a magnificent antelope.

But it's hard to argue that the ibex have been stressful on the Floridas' environment. And, unlike the oryx, they've remained within their original stocking range; as a mountain species, they are marooned on the Sky Island that is the Florida Mountains. They are reluctant to cross the surrounding basins to expand into other ranges. And, between hunting licenses (an out-of-state permit costs more than $1,000) and local food, lodging, and guide services, ibex contribute significantly to the state and local economy.

So until I'm given a reason to think otherwise, I'm happy they're here. Without the ibex, the Floridas would be just another desert mountain range among many similar ranges in the Basin and Range Province. But the ibex make the Floridas special.

I'll be back, with my binoculars—and more time and patience.

To Learn More

Read *The Mountains of New Mexico*, by Robert Julyan (Albuquerque: University of New Mexico Press, 2006).

AFTERWORD

Protecting Our History

As I was visiting the sites discussed in this book, I repeatedly was struck by how many sites had removable historic artifacts: airplane debris at the TWA crash site, old practice bomb casings at the World War II bomb targets, old tin cans at the homesteader cabins, turquoise fragments at Mount Chalchihuitl. In just a generation or two, souvenir hunters could conceivably remove all of these artifacts. New Mexico's physical historic record would be smudged or even erased.

Initially, in planning this book, I considered including a site where US soldiers had been ambushed by Apaches and where the combatants' graves remained, but an archaeologist friend said, "No, don't include *any* archaeological sites," because that would make them vulnerable to theft and desecration. As an archaeology volunteer myself, I didn't need convincing regarding sites that include pre-European remains—potsherds, lithics, ruins, and other items—but gravesites?

"I'm afraid so," the archaeologist said. Then he told me about souvenir hunters digging up soldiers' graves at Fort Craig to steal the dead soldiers' buttons, medals, armaments, personal effects—anything.

I was appalled—and I removed the ambush site from the list of topics for this book.

AFTERWORD

I tell this story only to underscore just how vulnerable many historic sites are, and just how unscrupulous and shameless the scoundrels who would despoil them.

I also want to enlist your help in protecting these sites. With some exceptions, I don't believe the answer lies in keeping the sites hidden from public view. Most of them are already widely known, and besides, looters are probably far more knowledgeable about their locations than the general public. Sadly, a certain neighbor of mine was a metal-detector enthusiast, and he knew exactly where to search for military artifacts.

No, the answer is for the rest of us to adopt a sense of stewardship regarding the sites. The major government land-management agencies such as the Bureau of Land Management and the Forest Service already have official site-steward programs for archaeological and other sites. I recommend these programs highly; they're a great opportunity to get outdoors and learn more about our history.

But even if we don't join one of these programs, we can become site stewards in a larger sense, "owning" the sites as if they were our personal property, which indeed they are, and reporting problems to the appropriate agencies. In fact, I recommend getting to know the archaeologists and paleontologists and historians at these agencies. They need the information you can provide, and once they know you and trust you they'll share information with you as well.

Once while hiking in the Jemez Mountains I came across pot hunters digging in a ruin atop a mesa. I crept away and hastened to notify someone. Unfortunately, this was before cell phones, and I doubt that law enforcement was able to respond to the theft in time. Nonetheless, there was something extremely satisfying in playing a role in trying to bust the bastards.

One problem we face in protecting historic sites is compartmentalizing what we view as worth saving. People who would never disturb an Ancestral Puebloan midden heap might plunder a homestead dump filled with tin cans and old bottles, saying, "That's just a bunch of junk." Yet the historic and archaeological value of the "junk" can be as high or higher than that of a Chacoan potsherd.

And for the record, the federal land-management agencies have established an age of fifty years as the cutoff age for defining "cultural artifacts." Accordingly, a beer bottle tossed in 1965 is now a cultural artifact and should not be removed from where it happens to be lying. That's how it must be: think of the historic value of a liquor bottle tossed in 1865.

Communities of Interests

Another way to become more knowledgeable about New Mexico's historic sites is to join a historical society. They have meetings and publish newsletters; members are able to answer your questions, and they often organize field trips. Probably the largest is the Historical Society of New Mexico, but there are more localized groups as well, such as the Albuquerque Historical Society and the Historical Society for Southeastern New Mexico; such groups exist in almost every county and town. There are also specialized societies such as the New Mexico Genealogical Society, the New Mexico Jewish Historical Society, and many more.

There are also archaeological groups, such as the New Mexico Archaeological Society and the Albuquerque Archaeological Society. They interpret archaeology broadly and include in their discussions post-European sites, such as missions.

As for hiking, there are several local and statewide guidebooks. Land-management agencies such as the Forest Service, the Bureau of Land Management, and the National Park Service can also provide guidebooks. Community groups such as senior and multigenerational centers sponsor hikes. The New Mexico Wilderness Alliance, a private group, has published guides to exploring the state's many wilderness areas, where historic sites often are located. There are many active Meetup groups centered on hiking.

And finally, you can also create your own network of likeminded souls. I once thought of myself as fairly unique in my

AFTERWORD

fondness for tracking down little-known features of history and geography, but I've since realized I'm part of a vast but unorganized community of people who also love exploration and discovery, whether searching for sharks' teeth in the Rio Puerco valley, a meteorite shatter cone in the Santa Fe Mountains, unmarked Spanish missions, Paleo-Indian sites, or old mining camps.

I never cease to marvel at the good fortune that brought me to New Mexico more than thirty years ago. Now you're here too, whether as a visitor or a permanent resident. I hope to meet you on the trail sometime. We'll have much to talk about.

TO LEARN MORE

As I wrote in the introduction, I've wanted to inspire you to get out and explore New Mexico's history on your own, whether off-road or not. To help you with this, I've compiled the following select list of resources I feel would enrich your travels. Please realize that the following list is by no means comprehensive; new guides are published each year, and many are excellent. These are simply the ones I've found useful over the years.

Roadside New Mexico: A Guide to Historic Markers, revised and expanded edition, by David Pike (Albuquerque: University of New Mexico Press, 2015). These markers are ubiquitous throughout the state, and we usually just whiz by them en route to somewhere else. That's too bad, because each of them suggests a story, and in this well-written and richly illustrated book the talented writer David Pike tells the full story behind each of them. The newly revised edition includes the markers recently added to commemorate women.

The Place Names of New Mexico, revised edition, by Robert Julyan (Albuquerque: University of New Mexico Press, 1996). An invaluable dictionary of the state's history and geography, giving the origins, meanings, folklore, and stories behind more than seven thousand named places: towns, villages, post offices, abandoned settlements, forts, mountains, rivers, lakes—you name it.

TO LEARN MORE

New Mexico: A New Guide to the Colorful State, by Lance Chilton et al. (Albuquerque: University of New Mexico Press, 1984). This is perhaps my favorite New Mexico guide, covering all the state's regions and not just the Rio Grande corridor and written with insight and depth. It's long out of print, but copies can still be found and are worth looking for.

New Mexico Then and Now, by William Stone, with text by Jerold G. Widdison (Englewood, CO: Westcliffe Publishers, 2003). The contemporary photos were deliberately taken from the same perspective as the old photos, dramatically showing the changes that have occurred during the intervening years. Interesting text gives context to the historic sites.

New Mexico Historical Biographies, by Don Bullis (Los Ranchos, NM: Rio Grande Books, 2011). An essential resource for anyone interested in New Mexico history. Bullis covers the broad span of the state's history, from the colonial period to the modern era. He is currently preparing an encyclopedia of the state's history.

Guide to the Hiking Areas of New Mexico, by Mike Hill (Albuquerque: University of New Mexico Press, 1995). Long out of print, this remains the most comprehensive guide to hiking in the state.

Hiking New Mexico, 3rd edition, by Laurence Parent (Guilford, CT: Falcon Guides, 2014). An excellent guide, with photographs by the author, to well-known and not-so-well-known hikes throughout New Mexico.

New Mexico's Wilderness Areas: The Complete Guide, by Bob Julyan, with photographs by Tom Till (Englewood, CO: Westcliffe Publishers, 1998). This book covers the entire state from the far southwest to the far north. While the status of some areas has changed since publication, the hiking information remains valid.

TO LEARN MORE

The Mountains of New Mexico, by Robert Julyan, with photographs by Carl Smith (Albuquerque: University of New Mexico Press, 2006). In addition to geology and natural history, this comprehensive book includes historic and cultural information about each of New Mexico's many mountains and ranges, many of which are little known.

New Mexico Road and Recreation Atlas (Santa Barbara, CA: Benchmark Maps, 2012). Unlike other road atlases to New Mexico, the maps in this one have been field checked. It's my personal favorite road atlas. For hikers, the land-status maps are especially useful.

Roadside History of New Mexico, by Francis L. Fugate and Roberta B. Fugate (Missoula, MT: Mountain Press, 1989). This book has always yielded unexpected information about New Mexico.

Anything by Richard Melzer. From the Fred Harvey houses to New Mexico cemeteries and graves to the Civilian Conservation Corps to Spanish colonial history to much more—there's hardly an aspect of New Mexico history to which this respected historian and talented author has not turned his attention.